The
Year
of the
Poet VI

January 2019

The Poetry Posse

inner child press, ltd.

I0149603

The Poetry Posse 2019

Gail Weston Shazor

Shareef Abdur Rasheed

Teresa E. Gallion

hülya n. yılmaz

Kimberly Burnham

Tzemin Ition Tsai

Elizabeth Esguerra Castillo

Jackie Davis Allen

Joe Paire

Caroline 'Ceri' Nazareno

Ashok K. Bhargava

Alicja Maria Kuberska

Swapna Behera

William S. Peters, Sr.

General Information

The Year of the Poet VI
January 2019 Edition

The Poetry Posse

1st Edition : 2019

This Publishing is protected under Copyright Law as a "Collection". All rights for all submissions are retained by the Individual Author and or Artist. No part of this Publishing may be Reproduced, Transferred in any manner without the prior **WRITTEN CONSENT** of the "Material Owners" or its Representative Inner Child Press. Any such violation infringes upon the Creative and Intellectual Property of the Owner pursuant to International and Federal Copyright Laws. Any queries pertaining to this "Collection" should be addressed to Publisher of Record.

Publisher Information
1st Edition : Inner Child Press
intouch@innerchildpress.com
www.innerchildpress.com

This Collection is protected under U.S. and International Copyright Laws

Copyright © 2019 : The Poetry Posse

ISBN-13 : 978-1-970020-72-4 (inner child press, ltd.)

$ 12.99

WHAT WOULD LIFE BE WITHOUT A LITTLE POETRY?

$\mathcal{D}$edication

This Book is dedicated to

Poetry . . .

The Poetry Posse

past, present & future

our Patrons and Readers

the Spirit of our Everlasting Muse

&

the Power of the Pen

to effectuate change!

In the darkness of my life
I heard the music
I danced . . .
and the Light appeared
and I dance

Janet P. Caldwell

Table of Contents

The Poetry Posse

Table of Contents . . . *continued*

January Featured Poets   93

$\mathcal{F}$oreword

Poetry can change the world. Words, language, all the ways to communicate with and listen to each other can transform the world, as we know it. There is so much to learn from the way an individual, a community, or language group uses words.

For example, the words for peace and war are very similar "odriyohdęda²ǫh" (war) and "odriyohsręda²ǫh" (peace) in Cayuga, a Native American language spoken in Canada. The government is trying to preserve the language and culture but there are less than 80 fluent speakers left. Peace "Odriyohsręda²ǫh" literally means the war has laid down or finished. For native speakers the words create an image, perhaps of men laying weapons down or a symbolic "war" laying down in a field where crops can once again be planted and children can grow.

Each of the world's seven or eight thousand languages creates different images, evokes diverse emotions, and carries a unique cultural significance.

In 2019 the Poets of the Inner Child Poetry Posse will breathe life into words creating a kind of visual poetry, arranging the letters to reflect each poet's inner voice manifested on the page while honoring the languages and cultures of many people around the world as well as our own diverse ancestry.

Each month we will visit a different region of the world, finding what is often stunningly beautiful, sometimes tragic and emotion-laden but always insightful and thought provoking. This year as our words journey across the pages and into the world we honor the United Nations which has declared 2019 the International Year of Indigenous Languages.

This month let your eyes ...

"anuhtunyu" (rejoice or adopt peace of mind) in Oneida spoken in the Great Lakes region
"ilihá:lon" (awaken, opening one's eyes from sleep) in Kosati spoken in Louisiana and Texas, US
"dseekshyaaksh" (strut or walk with a flair) in Shm'algyack spoken in Alaska, US
"dladáal" (stroll or walk slowly) in Haida spoken in British Columbia, Canada
"máñi" (travel or journey) in Ioway-Otoe-Missouria spoken in Kansas, US
"ji-k'ein" (jump around) in Tlingit spoken in the Pacific Northwest of North America
"tc'īgagō" (run) in Jacarilla Apache or Eastern Apache spoken in the North America
"nəpə̀mkawɑ" (walk or travel) in Abenaki-Penobscot spoken in Maine, US and Quebec, Canada

"zdocumb" (dance) in the Nanticoke Dialect of Massachusetts, US

... across the pages of this book, a tribute to Native American languages and cultures.

Kimberly Burnham, Ph.D.

Poets, Writers . . . know that we are the enchanting magicians that nourishes the seeds of dreams and thoughts . . . it is our words that entice the hearts and minds of others to believe there is something grand about the possibilities that life has to offer and our words tease it forth into action . . . for you are the Poet, the Writer to whom the Gift of Words has been entrusted . . .

~ wsp

$\mathcal{P}$reface

Dear Family and Friends,

Yes I am excited? This year we have aligned our vision with that of UNESCO as it honors and acknowledges a variety of Global Indigenous cultures. We are now in our sixth year of publication. As we are hitting another milestone, needless to say, I am elated. Our initial vision was to just perform at this level for the year of 2014. Since that time we have had the blessed opportunity to include many other wonderful word artists and storytellers in the Poetry Posse from lands, cultures and persuasions all over the world. We have featured hundreds of additional poets, thereby introducing their poetic offerings to our vast global readership.

In keeping with our effort and vision to expand the awareness of poets from all walks by making this offerings accessible, we at Inner Child Press International will continue to make every volume a FREE Download. The books are also available for purchase at the affordable cost of $7.00 per volume.

In the previous years, our monthly themes were Flowers, Birds, Gemstones, Trees and Past

Cultures. This year we have elected to continue the Cultural theme. In each month's volume you will have the opportunity to not only read at least one poem themed by our Poetry Posse members about such culture, but we have included a few words about the culture in our prologue. The reasoning behind this is that now our poetry has the opportunity to be educational for not only the reader, but we poets as well. We hope you find the poetic offerings insightful as we use our poetic form to relay to you what we too have learned through our research in making our offering available to you, our readership.

In closing, we would like to thank you for being an integral part of our amazing journey.

Enjoy our amazing featured poets . . . they are amazing!

Building Cultural Bridges of Understanding . . .

Bless Up

From the home in our hearts to yours

Bill
The Poetry Posse
Inner Child Press Ineternational

PS

Do Not forget about the World Healing, World Peace Poetry effort.

Available here

www.worldhealingworldpeacepoetry.com

**For Free Downloads of Previous Issues of
The Year of the Poet**

www.innerchildpress.com/the-year-of-the-poet

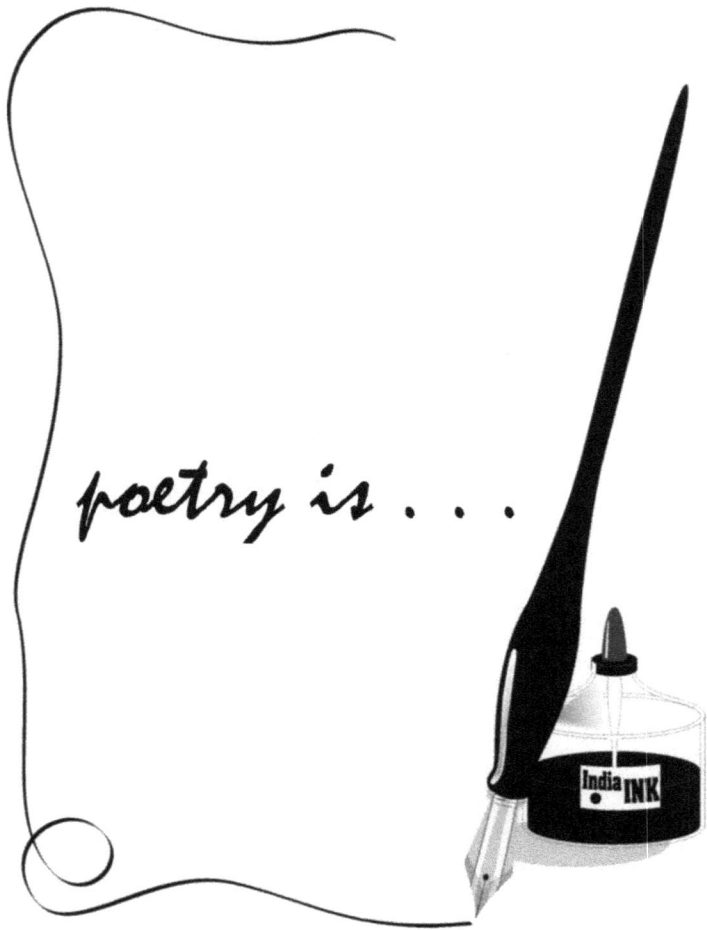

poetry is . . .

Indigenous North Americans

The unfortunate aspect of American history that is taught within our education systems is that it is heavily laden with lies, deceits and misinformation that shades or distorts the truth. This month, January 2019, we *The Poetry Posse* at *The Year of the Poet* are excited to present to you through our poetry a variant version of perspective through our poetry. We hope you find our work insightful and contemplative.

For more information visit
https://en.wikipedia.org/wiki/Indigenous_peoples_of_the_Americas

Poets . . .
sowing seeds in the
Conscious Garden of Life,
that those who have yet to come
may enjoy the Flowers.

The
Year
of the
Poet VI

January 2019

The Poetry Posse

Poetry succeeds where instruction fails.

~ wsp

Gail Weston Shazor

This is a creative promise ~ my pen will speak to and for the world. Enamored with letters and respectful of their power, I have been writing for most of my life. A mother, daughter, sister and grandmother I give what I have been given, greatfilledly.

Author of . . .

"An Overstanding of an Imperfect Love"
&
Notes from the Blue Roof

Lies My Grandfathers Told Me

available at Inner Child Press.

www.facebook.com/gailwestonshazor
www.innerchildpress.com/gail-weston-shazor
navypoet1@gmail.com

Bovoni Blues

The
Dump is
Burgeoning
Under the weight
Of left behinds from
Hurricanes that passed
On their own tropical tours
Of the unlucky Antilles
When paradise suspended quickly
And each person's life was forever changed
Our left behinds mounted up quickly
Returning home, we began sorting
The broken memories from tears
As the mound of yesterdays
Rising too quickly
The black sentinel,
Bovoni, stood
Quietly
In the
Dust

Single Shot Scotch

Scared, the bottle swung free from discontent
Cheaper than deserved for a gift
But it never lasts long, this wet fear
In one drop of clarity, he breathes
Protecting the daughter and the wife
And even the son corrupted and dying slowly
In this world of darkness

Tear filled glass brimming
The impotence of that moment
Is split by decisions taken
Without a proper reference to life
A color-filled rage trying to justify
Single messages on the airwaves
And he is dying slowly trying to be pure

Cheap scotch splashes
Into a Styrofoam cup slowly
Courage and determination rule the night
Plastic impersonations rule the day
A mortgage and dreams rule his life
And he is never satisfied being
A half-cocked cop

It was not that he hated anyone
Save himself, save what he was
The dram bound the trigger
Taught in his hand and mind
The pebble sounded a cannon
Much like the pea under the mattress
The single shot scotch changed him forever

Death comes to the Farm

Daylight and dark
The earth turns in infinitum
And we make choices
So why move my feet
When I can do nothing
To stop this turning

The photos are laid side by side
Witnessing the carnage
Of man's fall from grace
Wounds open wide
Scars not yet formed
In a semblance of normalcy

That is anything but normal
The rage of impotence
At not being master
Of the animals on the earth
And not realizing
That we all are animals

From earth to earth
And dust to dust
The blood spilled calls out
From the surface of the dirt
And we are left to wonder
Just who is the keeper of who

Alicja Maria Kuberska

.

Alicja Maria Kuberska – awarded Polish poetess, novelist, journalist, editor. She was born in 1960, in Świebodzin, Poland. She now lives in Inowrocław, Poland.

In 2011 she published her first volume of poems entitled: "The Glass Reality". Her second volume "Analysis of Feelings", was published in 2012. The third collection "Moments" was published in English in 2014, both in Poland and in the USA. In 2014, she also published the novel - "Virtual roses" and volume of poems "On the border of dream". Next year her volume entitled "Girl in the Mirror" was published in the UK and "Love me" , " (Not)my poem" in the USA. In 2015 she also edited anthology entitled "The Other Side of the Screen".

In 2016 she edited two volumes: "Taste of Love" (USA), "Thief of Dreams" (Poland) and international anthology entitled " Love is like Air" (USA). In 2017 she published volume entitled "View from the window" (Poland). She also edits series of anthologies entitled "Metaphor of Contemporary" (Poland)

Her poems have been published in numerous anthologies and magazines in Poland, the USA, the UK, Albania, Belgium, Chile, Spain, Israel, Canada, India, Italy, Uzbekistan, Czech Republic, South Korea and Australia. She was a featured poet of New Mirage Journal (USA) in the summer of 2011.

Alicja Kuberska is a member of the Polish Writers Associations in Warsaw, Poland and IWA Bogdani, Albania. She is also a member of directors' board of Soflay Literature Foundation.

Karol May and Indians

In prison, a draft reminds about the existence of wind.
Air stands in the small space of the clink, it became stifling
Behind the bars, in the window glass, the sky changes
shades
Sometimes the sun sends a few rays to the cold cell

Thoughts break out to freedom and vast plains
to the world where factory sirens do not exist,
the starry sky is not veiled by the dark smoke,
and where the swinging grasses hum songs about warriors.

A man can escape from reality and start to live in a teepee.
-abadon the gray walls and the footsteps of the guard
behind the door,
hide on a prairie full of herd of bison
and gallop ahead on the back of a wild horse

The Great Manitou takes in the lost wanderers.
Old Shatterhand gives a helping hand to the weaver's son
and leads him in the front of the great chief of Apache
Confused blood sealed eternal brotherhood

The time has stopped on the written sheets of paper.
The heroic Indians are reborn in the novel
The eagle feathers are draped in their black hair.
The shaman's prolonged singing is heard far away.

An old mirror

When I walk into the house
The old mirror wakes up.
It winks knowingly with a big, glass eye.
On the other side I can see a girl that I know.

It always faithfully accompanies the passing time
And reflects transience in the shimmering silver sheet.
I suspect that it harbors all faces
But it is discreetly silent and it guards entrusted secrets.

It survived the conflagration of a revolution, turmoil of
war.
Unstable and fragile, it remembers many owners.
We are together and we catch fleeting moments

My Village Borow

I no longer have a nest here
But I come back, like a swallow,
To places of my childhood.

I wander the sandy hedgerows,
To participate in the mystery of lark song.
I arrange bouquets
Of wild poppies and cornflowers -
And raise up to the clouds.

Old trees, to which I confided my secrets,
Still grow,
Tart, wild cherries
And sweet-scented linden
As once -
I divine the world in the mirror of the lake.
I listen to the waves and the wind.

Apparently nothing has changed.
Only the cemetery hill,
Like a diary of life,
Is ever more clear

Jackie Davis Allen

Jackie Davis Allen, otherwise known as Jacqueline D. Allen or Jackie Allen, grew up in the Cumberland Mountains of Appalachia. As the next eldest daughter of a coal miner father and a stay at home mother, she was the first in her family to attend and graduate from college. Her siblings, in their own right, are accomplished, though she is the only one, to date, that has discovered the gift of writing.

Graduating from Radford University, with a Bachelors of Science degree in Early Education, she taught in both public and private schools. For over a decade she taught private art classes to children both in her home and at a local Art and Framing Shop where she also sold her original soft sculptured Victorian dolls and original christening gowns.

She resides in northern Virginia with her husband, taking much needed get-aways to their mountain home near the Blue Ridge Mountains, a place that evokes memories of days spent growing up in the Appalachian Mountains.

A lover of hats, she has worn many. Following marriage to her college sweetheart, and as wife, mother, grandmother, teacher, tutor, artist, writer, poet and crafter, she is a lover of art and antiques, surrounding herself, always, with books, seeking to learn more.

In 2015 she authored *Looking for Rainbows, Poetry, Prose and Art*, and in 2017, *Dark Side of the Moon*. Both books of mostly narrative poetry were published by Inner Child Press and were edited by hulya n. yilmaz.

http://www.innerchildpress.com/jackie-davis-allen.php
jackiedavisallen.com

Rooted in Native Belief

Long have I been told, a story, one handed down
By relatives. An oral one. No documents to corroborate,
That my long deceased NC and TN paternal relatives
Had in fact, descended from the Cherokee Indians.
They concentrated, living in the same geographic areas.

Whether true or not, the current political situation
Would have me to keep quiet. And, yet, contrary
To not being proud, I have no need to jump
Onto a bandwagon, nor any need to submit my DNA
As proof or not; nothing to gain either way.

All I can say, by way of the matter, is that a paternal aunt,
Born in the early 1900s, informed me before she passed,
That she believed it true. Witness: the family's high
Cheekbones. The straight, dark hair of my father.
He little needing to shave, little facial hair.

In 1923, two weeks prior to her Christmas day, 35th
Birthday, my father's mother passed away, leaving behind
Nine children. My father's father, both from memory, and
In photos, appears as a brave, resilient Cherokee, like an
Indian Chief. He passed in the 1970s. In his mid 90s.

So, one might inquire, if I am, indeed, a descendant
Of the Native American Cherokees, how is it that I,
My siblings, my mother, and her father, we have such
Abundant, naturally curly hair? A better question, to pose,
Perhaps, is, whether or not I am being true to who I am.

Dreams

He went to the brink.
He went to the edge.
He went to a busy town near his home.
He went only in his dreams, went rushing,
Looking for that which he hoped to find.

He dreamed lofty dreams,
Higher than the sky.
He dreamed at night, found them filled with treasures.
He even dreamed during the daylight hours,
Searching for something grand to pave his way.

He went to school both day and night,
Found that it was cold, it was hot,
Discovered that rewards were difficult
Though not beyond his means.
For dangling before him was the coveted prize.

He walked. He ran.
He stumbled.
Stumped every one of his toes,
Skinned his knees, then prayed.
Praying relief, he fell down on his knees.

Oh, yes. He went to the edge.
He went beyond. He traveled, then, to the towns,
To the cities and discovered that from working hard,
And holding high his principles, his ethics, therein
Dwelt the real possibility for fulfilling youthful dreams.

Let Us Come Together

Prayers floating through the air
On wings of nature's blessing.
Sing they out the olden songs,
> Of trials and tribulations, a people
> Who, long ago came by land and sea
> Holding in their hearts sad memories.

The pounding drumbeat of hearts
Syncopate into memory's past wrongs
Of long ago days, torn and faded.
> On pages recording passengers,
> Names found of sailing ships and crew
> Except for those considered property.

Theirs was a journey, borne on backs
Of heavy hearts, rendered and torn;
And, though they are no more, today
> Some are the descendants of those
> Who stole lives, they taking part
> Doing nothing to provide any relief.

Save the treasured remnants
Of our native customs and heritage!
Pave then a better path, a better way
> For all our nation's people; choose
> The right. Live in the light. Regardless
> Of race or color. Let us live in harmony.

Tzemin
Ition
Tsai

Dr. Tzemin Ition Tsai (蔡澤民博士) was born in Tzemin Ition Tsai Taiwan, Republic of China, in 1957. He holds a Ph.D. in Chemical Engineering and two Masters of Science in Applied Mathematics and Chemical Engineering. He is an associate professor at the Asia University (Taiwan), editor of "Reading, Writing and Teaching" academic text. He also writes the long-term columns for Chinese Language Monthly in Taiwan.

He is a scholar with a wide range of expertise, while maintaining a common and positive interest in science, engineering and literature member.

He has won many national literary awards. His literary works have been anthologized and published in books, journals, and newspapers in more than 40 countries and have been translated into more than a dozen languages.

American Dream

One gust of white smoke
Forty years, in a twinkling of an eye, disappeared
Meet again after such a long separation
Two old but refused to be dull faces
Full of childish eyes like before
No any bit of stubble residue
The wrinkles are mixed with two white and black eyebrows
Talking always about the old topic
old
No longer being disguised

One bowl of rice porridge
With marinated cabbage
The tears in the corners of the eyes are damp
How is it compared to onion sauerkraut hot dogs?
My old friend in high school
Only rely on the Ph. D. certificate in chemical engineering
Set off into the America world
Accomplished both success and fame
Among us
Second to none

One parting
The plane will take off and land tomorrow
You will return to the other side of the Pacific
Point your hand straight to the Golden Trumpet-tree at the
next door
Under the red tile roof is just the home of my parents
Why did it come this fall so not simply?
Those cicadas keep silence seems to be all dumb
That home in the other side of the Pacific is belong to my
son and grandsons
But did not know why
I have never written a poem for it

The Spring Breeze Never Knows How To Leave Feelings

Spring breeze blowing
The wind chimes follow jingle-jangle all the way
Maple leaves drift with it
Take away all my cares so frivolously
Spring breeze blowing
Agitate the flag on the sail
Steam above sea level whistling out like a roaring monster
The ocean that has been warmed up is rolling

Spring breeze has no willing to change
Looking around for whales hidden inside the ocean
The tracks that is difficult to track
Forget itself
In a fuzzy consciousness
Leave a hint of exclamation
When is the heart no longer hurt?

The sun sometimes fails to keep an appointment
Why is dark night sure to come every day?
Maybe you can find it under the moon
That course following the Big Dipper
Spring breeze always attracts a riot of spring here and there
You must always remember
Never lose
That footprint goes forward

The Call of Youth in The Moonlight

The window is wide open
The decayed trees in front are crying for the cold winter
that is about to leave
The bright moonlight is as usual
The low wall along the side of the yard with green buds
Firefly flying here and there
When we have
Gradually lost the consensus of childhood?
Different dreams of independent thinking
Youthful looks and dresses are not a patch on the laid-back
bear
Who has occupied the bed for over ten years

The night is deep
That childhood sweet girl with robe draped over the
shoulders and whispered
With a light voice could not be more lightly
Eyes of The childhood sweet boy standing against the
window
Cold eyes like a sword
Giggles
Can replace nothing in the belly full of ambition
Carefully listen
The swallow's spring humming have already
Broken out of the windows

Mist in endless whiteness
Let us embracing and sleep once again
As you and I met for the first time
In the mother's cradle
Dream pure hearts
The souls who promised us to bless each other

No longer my companion on this distant life road
Now that you have do not look back
Why bother the tears
Well up in your eyes?

Shareef
Abdur
Rasheed

Shareef Abdur-Rasheed, AKA Zakir Flo was born and raised in Brooklyn, New York. His education includes Brooklyn College, Suffolk County Community College and Makkah, Saudi Arabia. He is a Veteran of the Viet Nam era, where in 1969 he reverted to his now reverently embraced Islamic Faith. He is very active in the Islamic community and beyond with his teachings, activism and his humanity.

Shareef's spiritual expression comes through the persona of "Zakir Flo" . Zakir is Arabic for "To remind". Never silent, Shareef Abdur-Rasheed is always dropping science, love, consciousness and signs of the time in rhyme.

Shareef is the Patriarch of the Abdur-Rasheed Family with 9 Children (6 Sons and 3 Daughters) and 41 Grandchildren (24 Boys and 17 Girls).

For more information about Shareef, visit his personal FaceBook Page at :

https://www.facebook.com/shareef.abdurrasheed1
https://zakirflo.wordpress.com

forked tongue..,

likes of serpent
slithering low on earth
seeking prey, seeking
strike, overtake, devour
this was european
indigenous called him white
from time they appeared
what seemed out of nowhere
they were treated fair
native folk regardless
tribe, language spoke invoked
high principles instilled
through ancestors
dem knew, lived, loved, spoke
taught truth
universal laws from thee one
great spirit who created
earth, moon, sun
all things
established what is good, evil,
true, false
thousands of years before
europeans appeared
tribes like Nez Perce
french for pierced nose
although they call themselves
Niimiipuu the walking people
northwest country
chief joseph
(Him-mah-too-yah-lat-kekt)
thunder rolling down mountain
his father before him taught him

not to give up their land
no matter what
never trust them
europeans had eyes on that
to take what was not theirs
no said chief of Nez Perce
and so this same ol sameo
played out throughout
and we all know how that
panned out
indigenous people own
this land they call America
know this, understand it
native peoples are the rightful
heirs though many who know this
just don't care.
and these same folk invoke
words like justice
translates "Just-Us "
liberty and " Just-Us "
that's why ancestors said
" Never Trust. Never Trust "

food4thought = education

lower thy branch..,

are we as lofty as a mountain?
powerful as lightning, thunder
sun, moon, tsunami, monsoon?
makes one wonder or maybe
not
there are those who just go
without regard, just into self
by ' n ' large
dem don't take a look around
magnificent array of creation
on display
many dwarfs those who thought
all things should cater to them
needs, greed
dem never concede
wrapped up in the me..me..me
dem can't see, seee?
forest for trees
just everybody must do as i
please
but i thought we are all human
beings
so therefore seems awfully petty
what a pity
dem who ' A-T ' S#!+y
instead of gratitude for people
who care, sincere
they don't care, can't see, unaware
that's a privilege right there
instead at end of day
dem say " i'm privileged, entitled
only my needs are vital "

arrogance invites darkness,
humility light
we all have rights
first give them their rights
and for you
creator will make it all right
all day ' n ' night
me, me, me go away until one day
you reappear as ..we, we, we

food4thought = education

flesh 'n' blood..,

i am in need of help,
mercy in high demand
constantly fragile me
in need
thou art not an island unto
thyself
yes, your blessed have survived
countless test
but never the less mere mortal
has been afforded relief in times
of need
regardless what one may think
or our intention
in spite of our frailties
we overcome through
divine intervention
yes to this you, me, we
must attest, concede
look upon the signs and read
release oneself from the ' me '
open spiritual eyes to see
" MERCY " bestowed never earned,
never owed
you are totally dependent
don't be offended
as long as your life can be ended
it behooves one to choose one's
priorities wisely, succinctly
to whom one gives appreciation,
praise, devotion
when in spite of our finite status
MERCY intercedes
in spite of the fact
what one deserves is another thing

Kimberly Burnham

Find yourself in the pattern. As a 28-year-old photographer, Kimberly Burnham appreciated beauty. Then an ophthalmologist diagnosed her with a genetic eye condition saying, "Consider life, if you become blind." She discovered a healing path with insight, magnificence, and vision. Today, 33 years later, a poet and neurosciences expert with a PhD in Integrative Medicine, Kimberly's life mission is to change the global face of brain health. Using health coaching, Reiki, Matrix Energetics, craniosacral therapy, acupressure, and energy medicine, she supports people in their healing from brain, nervous system, and chronic pain issues. As managing editor of Inner Child Magazine, Kimberly's 2019 project is peace, language, and visionary poetry with her recently published book, *Awakenings: Peace Dictionary, Language and the Mind, a Daily Brain Health Program.*

http://www.NerveWhisperer.Solutions
https://www.linkedin.com/in/kimberlyburnham

Peace From Sea to Mountain

"Gyamgm'aatk" moon in Shm'algyack
a Native American language of Alaska
hangs over the sea
where young men harvest "gyantee" (sea cucumber)
and the waves roll "gya'galtk" (to roll)
"gya'wn" (now, today) as we stroll through the dictionary
taking a stab at peace and calm
"gyehlk" (to spear, stab)
"gyeksh (to be calm, peace)
feeling something will happen and change life for the better
"gyelkwsh" (to feel something will happen)
while hunting for berries in the mountains
"gyem" (Saskatoon berries)
"gyepsh" (hill, mountain, up high)
seeking high places as we learn more about the life
of words and hearts

A Peace of Attrition

The Canadian government is fighting
to keep Cayuga alive
only 79 fluent speakers know the words
"odriyohdęda?ǫh" war
and "odriyohsręda?ǫh" peace literally
the war has laid down or finished

Perhaps this war on words
killing languages everyday
will end when we lay down
aggressive words
arrogant words
hateful words
and words meant to silence another

Perhaps we will all speak the native tongues of our
ancestors
of our friends and family
and then learn the languages loved by those across the sea
when we raise up words of peace
"odriyohsręda?ǫh"
loving words
companionate words
and words meant to include everyone

Conlang Peace

If you made up a word
constructed a language (conlang)
for peace

What would you build
would it be full of gentle melodious vowels
or a consonant root
resembling a natural language

Would it be whimsical or utilitarian
easy to learn would it be
memorable and lasting
like the peace it describes
or have an S like "sérë"
or an R as in "rainë"
both peace in Tolkein's Elvish Quenya

Would it be more like "wayu" in Wasaqalu
or "paco" in Esperanto
Klingon for peace "roj"
or "panpi" in Lojban
"eace-pay" in Pig Latin

"Fpomtokx" or "aylrrtok"
peace in Na'vi a conlang
spoken by the people of Pandora
"e-wee-ne-tu" another movie word for peace
in Pocahontas resembling a Native American language
but made up all the same

Elizabeth E. Castillo

Elizabeth Esguerra Castillo is a multi-awarded and an Internationally-Published Contemporary Author/Poet and a Professional Writer / Creative Writer / Feature Writer / Journalist / Travel Writer from the Philippines. She has 2 published books, "Seasons of Emotions" (UK) and "Inner Reflections of the Muse", (USA). Elizabeth is also a co-author to more than 60 international anthologies in the USA, Canada, UK, Romania, India. She is a Contributing Editor of Inner Child Magazine, USA and an Advisory Board Member of Reflection Magazine, an international literary magazine. She is a member of the American Authors Association (AAA) and PEN International.

Web links:

Facebook Fan Page

https://free.facebook.com/ElizabethEsguerraCastillo

Google Plus

https://plus.google.com/u/0/+ElizabethCastillo

North American Yup'iks

Genuine people as their name implies
With "Yuk" as their language
Common ancestors of the Eskimos and Aleut
With their families spending spring and summer
At fish camp, joined by the others during winter.
The "qasqig" a communal men's house
Was the community's center for festivals and ceremonies
While the "ena", the traditional women's house was right
    next door.
Eclectic and exotic culture the Yu'piks lived with
Real people with wonderful origins.

Fragile

I have often seen innocent angels roaming the streets at
    night
Young vagabonds loitering dark alleys, scavengers
    searching for the light
Tattered clothes, soiled feet, with eyes that question their
    mere existence
Young bloods, lost souls in need of careful attention and
    sustenance.

Fragile bodies crossing the roads, stopping cars to beg for
    money
Abandoned by some ruthless families, in the dark they hide
    their agony,
Some abused, maltreated by society who should be the first
    to care
Fallen angels seeking for the truth behind their helpless
    state.

Famish, greasy children pitifully sleeping on the cold
    pavement
It was not their choice to be born and suffer in such sad
    predicament
Oh, God lay down your mercy on them and let them have
    the taste of life they were deprived
These precious one whom You adore, let your Light guide
    them and help them survive.

The River's Ebb and Flow

The water that flows freely
Symbolizes life that goes on continuously
Its beautiful ebb and flow
Caught up in circles but always brings a larger tomorrow.

The rhythmic sound the river water makes
A melodramatic scene when a leaf falls from a fragile
    branch of a tree,
And is carried away by the running water as if escaping its
    reality
While way up above, the sky meets the charismatic shadow
    of my reflection.

At night time, the river may seem still and emotionless
But its tranquility echoes even in the darkness
As the stars in the moonlit sky bathes in their own images
    on the water
In the depths of deafening silence, the flow of time goes
inevitably.

The river teaches us the art of holding on and letting go,
But it also sends a subtle message of just going with the
flow
For if we force our way against the strong current
We may stumble at the wrong direction and hurt ourselves
    in the end.

Joe
Paire

Joe Paire

Joseph L Paire' aka Joe DaVerbal Minddancer . . .
is a quiet man, born in a time where civil liberties
were a walk on thin ice. He's been a victim of his
own shyness often sidelined in his own quest for
love. He became the observer, charting life's path.
Taking note of the why, people do what they do.
His writings oft times strike a cord with the
dormant strings of the reader. His pen the rosined
bow drawn across the mind. He comes full-frontal
or in the subtlest way, always expressing in a way
that stimulate the senses.

https://www.facebook.com/joe.minddancer

Maiden America

What land is this that lays before me
Undefined by borders of those who explore me
It's peaceful here with plenty to go around
The people here have adapted to the sound
Drum beats speak of food and weather
places to teach the young and gather
We only need just one

Different tribes with similar values
from the tip of the north and southern bayous
Indigenous people keep your values high
Influence comes by the belief of lies
All these cultural achievements and beauty
Every facet of society had its duty
We only need just one

Hundreds, thousands, millions of years
With the smoke from muskets it began to disappear
This land is our land, this land was your land
Torn from sure hands stolen by con men
No one saw the harm then
There was plenty for all men
We only need just one

Made in, not by Americans
Genocide of Native Americans
Faded Americans jaded Americans
Slaved in Americans paved in Americans
The British are coming, the British are coming
The sounds of the drums just stopped
We only need just one was dropped

The Scent Of Nature

Heavenly smells of holiday kitchens
A crawling toddler whose scent I won't mention
How does Grandma know it's going to rain?
How do you know that meal has gone lame?

Oh my goodness what is that smell
Oysters on the half shell and love in the air is thick
We know what you were doing
with that redeye mind trick

Downwind with a bow and arrow
Caught with the cry of a sparrow
The ocean is near
This potion is cleared for the tasting

I can tell where you've been
I can smell where you've been
Where the hell have you been
Does this smell right to you?

MMM someone's having a bar b que
Someone's got some new perfume
Ode' de New Car in June
MMM new leather too, Dude! What did you do?

Give me a spring day of full blooms
Give me Jazz in a smoke-filled room
Home fries and bacon garlic and maybe
Cinnamon toast with some fresh roast coffee

Don't artificially mock me
The Scent of Nature adopts me

Day Number One

I'm quitting this and starting that
I'm building a regiment and will stick to it
Withdrawals and soreness
Sweating and hoarseness
I can't venture off coarse just;
I can skip tomorrow, can't I?
Day two and the plan dies
Refund on a treadmill
We run for the peppermill
This is going to taste good
"I know I could, I know I could"

Day one and the sweat pours
Why am I thinking about petit fours
What's the score of my weight
Why the chore for my weight
I have a taste, for a taste for
Who do I abase my case for
Day two and the plan dies
I can barely move these sore thighs
Just a drag, just a puff
just a sip, it's not enough
Will power, DO YOUR STUFF

Two weeks in and meat taste funny
Smaller clothing doesn't cost less money!
I'm resting better
But I never truly lost any weight
I'm actually in line for a nice buffet
I thought about a change I found something better
Day one of just doing me forever

hülya
n.
yılmaz

A retired Liberal Arts professor, hülya n. yılmaz [sic] is Co-Chair and Director of Editing Services at Inner Child Press International, and a literary translator. Her poetry has been published in an excess of sixty anthologies of global endeavors. Two of her poems are permanently installed in *TelePoem Booth*, a nation-wide public art exhibition in the U.S. She has shared her work in Kosovo, Canada, Jordan and Tunisia. hülya has been honored with a 2018 WIN Award of British Colombia, Canada. She is presently working on three poetry books and a short-story collection. hülya finds it vital for everyone to understand a deeper sense of self and writes creatively to attain a comprehensive awareness for and development of our humanity.

hülya n. yılmaz, Ph.D.

Writing Web Site
https://hulyanyilmaz.com/

Editing Web Site
https://hulyasfreelancing.com/

Cherokee to Ho-Chunk

it is not only the volume as far as their names
but also their inherent cultures' vast and timeless bounty
that made today's North America, the supposedly
newly discovered world's 3rd largest continent

and, each of their tribes suffered
Native Americans, that is
they faced pain beyond
humanity's capacity
they were subjected to tortures
to butchery, to slavery and to conversion
to Christianity – or else, they would have met death

we all sit now in our own comfort on their land
having pushed them into the most remote
corners of low lands of their country
either pitying what has become of them over time
or admiring their enduring strength, integrity, dignity
how, amid immensely bloody tragedies, they still do rise
to shout loud and act out their ancient words of wisdom
as to how to live with respect for every dab of our world
in honor of not merely the two-legged animal species
but, of our four-legged counterparts, too

regardless of what any of us has / not done in person
collectively, we bear the onerous weight of annihilating
an entire indigenous people, together with their languages,
cultures, generations-surviving rich history and daily lives;
of guiding them to their irreparable shameful demise

how many times have i cited your wise insights
not having a clue whom to give the credit to

dear members of the Cherokee, the Apache,
the Iroquois, the Pawnee people, the Sioux,
the Miwok, the Shoshone, the Osage Nation,
the Navajo, the Lakota people, the Ute people,
the Sauk people, the Cheyenne, the Crow Nation,
the Nez Perce people, the Ho-Chunk, the Ponca,
the Paiute, the Omaha people, the Hidatsa, the Odawa,
the Chumash people, the Mandan, the Duwamish people,
the Iowa people, the Cahuilla, the Modoc people, the Otoe,
the Yakama, the Pima people, the Chiricahua, the Arikara,
the Missouria, the Sac and Fox Nation, the Omaha people,
the Meskwaki, the Odawa, the Washoe people, the Patwin,
the Goshute, the Serrano people, the Maidu, the Quechan,
the Oneida Indian Nation, the Yankton Sioux Tribe,
the Kumeyaay, the Indigenous peoples of the Northwest,
the Chinookan peoples, the Clatsop, the Miami people,
the Tulalip, the Mandan, Hidatsa and Arikara Nation,
the Confederated Salish and Kootenai Tribes . . .

forgive my silence
forgive my ignorance
i bow before each of you
forgive my daring, desperate plea
that which i brought along with me
in my quest to seek wisdom from thee
it is said to come from a Plains Indian, you see:

"Give me knowledge, so I may have kindness for all."

ignorance

a woman of Turkish birth
who in other words should know better
having been born into the same region and religion
having received, though with some interruption
her early, mid-level and high school education
in an equally Islamic country
regardless of any variation

after settling in North America
coming to terms with Islam, its women and men
within the pre-scribed rigid boundaries of her schooling
she determinedly sought
the highest possible form of education
for her own sake, to the point to be able to
expose unilaterally
all that which aims to confine the female territory
in their public sphere but also in that of their privacy
years passed
in fact, decades were gone
her lifelong passion for poetry
accompanied her to the Middle East
Jordan was the first stop-nation on her route
a festival of festivals took her to the city of Jerash
the amazingly intact, world's awe Roman Amphitheater
offered to the first night of poems a fairy-tale-like home
poets from across the globe joined in the shared breathing
of the magically fresh air
for the furthering of their inspiration

a gloriously triumphant, one-of-a-kind
celebration took place
this timeless art surpassed
any and all potential limitation of space

it gracefully accompanied
the mesmerizing dance steps of the old
a breathtakingly melodic language
introduced the many verses
in a soothingly gentle, sweetest
and an intoxicating embrace
a rarest form of a jubilant friendship swayed in mid-air
and dashed about, hand in hand, with mutual wonder
patting the poets' ink into a forthright admiration

the same ignorant female
inhaled every precious hug in a child's utter awe
throughout the following festival days and nights
contemplating all along, how she could live without . . .
Al-Karak was for some poets the last stop
the regal beauty of the valleys and the mountains
along the way to the Castle of histories, long passed
astonished her out of her ignorance of the past
the Domed Stable from the Ottoman Era
graciously welcomed the visibly inspired souls
more poems attained their momentarily-lasting fame
as continuous readings met a vigorous applause
her breath was taken away
as unconditional love for the poetic art
and for each with a passion to compose it
filled the air in eager and plentiful abundance

there stood a preciously tender plate of a kind of affection
she had never expected, or could have imagined
to live before

under her hat as the former ignorant witness . . .
she thus dove
peacefully into love
and divine acceptance

hülya n. yılmaz

an honor-killing prey

in the hope-filled dreams for our children
we were once one as we had eternally been
living the privilege of a fertile womb
for eons in its rightfully safe haven
with a promise to an offspring

you however are no longer

i met you again in your tragedy

at the sight of the butchery of your yet-to blossom life
and that of the treasured one inside you to love and to adore
the internal pump on my left thus burnt its reddest at its
core

the same decade
though in a different space
may have very well left intact
your innocently loving youthful grace

i now mourn your brutally wasted precious being
while i wish to have been a home-bound kin to you
though we had for long lost each other's caring touch
as we were put on foreign tract to relate only from afar
i remain with the hope to have arrived somewhat on time
to gather up my courage to opt to keep your final breath
ajar

Teresa E. Gallion

Teresa E. Gallion was born in Shreveport, Louisiana and moved to Illinois at the age of 15. She completed her undergraduate training at the University of Illinois Chicago and received her master's degree in Psychology from Bowling Green State University in Ohio. She retired from New Mexico state government in 2012.

She moved to New Mexico in 1987. While writing sporadically for many years, in 1998 she started reading her work in the local Albuquerque poetry community. She has been a featured reader at local coffee houses, bookstores, art galleries, museums, libraries, Outpost Performance Space, the Route 66 Festival in 2001 and the State of Oklahoma's Poetry Festival in Cheyenne, Oklahoma in 2004. She occasionally hosts an open mic.

Teresa's work is published in numerous Journals and anthologies. She has two CDs: *On the Wings of the Wind* and *Poems from Chasing Light*. She has published three books: *Walking Sacred Ground, Contemplation in the High Desert* and *Chasing Light*.

Chasing Light was a finalist in the 2013 New Mexico/Arizona Book Awards.

The surreal high desert landscape and her personal spiritual journey influence the writing of this Albuquerque poet. When she is not writing, she is committed to hiking the enchanted landscapes of New Mexico. You may preview her work at

http://bit.ly/1aIVPNq or *http://bit.ly/13IMLGh*

Sandia Pueblo Fiesta

The natives move to the beat
of sacred drums.
The rhythms embedded in DNA strands
flowing for a thousand sunsets
reach the feet of today.

Every bell, every feather, every fox tail
symbolizes a piece of natural order
of all things native
from generation to generation.

They dance to remember,
to pay homage, to pass tradition
to the next generation of legs and feet
stirring the high desert sand.

The chant in sync with the drumbeat
enthralls the crowd of bystanders
caught in the rapture of sound.
It is an ancient universal call.

This Door

Heavy walnut is the composition.
Strident marble pinches its way
through cracks and crevices
A stained yellow has turned away
from innocence over millenium.

This door's story is intimate
and it does not tell its secrets.
Those marks, bruises and
irregular shades of color
tease the brainstems of two
youthful lads standing before the door
waiting for permission to enter.
They pass the time in competition
of who has the best imagination.

Genghis Khan laid his blade on this door.
No, the California earthquake bounced
it on the concrete.
No, Jesus opened this door to enter the temple.
No, the monsoons warped this door
at the Maharaja's Palace.
No, the slaves opened this door to greet guests
in the antebelum south.

Suddenly the door opened wide.
The Guru says, *yes you lads were participants*
in the history of this door.
You are very old souls.
Enter with open hearts and minds.
I will tell you stories tonight.

Winter is Coming

Fall is letting go of its
golden lace and greets brown.
Airstreams blow close to the ground.
Brown leaves run in front of the wind.

The cottonwoods get naked
and show off their character.
It is a perennial fashion revue
of trees with great curves.

Every tree has a branch
flexing its muscles with
eyepopping sexiness
that captivates our sensors.

Each transition of seasons,
we are given a show
of nature's splendor
as it dazzles us in winter's light.

Ashok K. Bhargava

Ashok Bhargava is a poet, writer, community activist, public speaker, management consultant and a keen photographer. Based in Vancouver, he has published several collections of his poems: Riding the Tide, Mirror of Dreams, A Kernel of Truth, Skipping Stones, Half Open Door and Lost in the Morning Calm. His poetry has been published in various literary magazines and anthologies.

Ashok is a Poet Laureate and poet ambassador to Japan, Korea and India. He is founder of WIN: Writers International Network Canada. Its main objective is to inspire, encourage, promote and recognize writers of diverse genres, artists and community leaders. He has received many accolades including Nehru Humanitarian Award for his leadership of Writers International Network Canada, Poets without Borders Peace Award for his journeys across the globe to celebrate peace and to create alliances with poets, and Kalidasa Award for creative writings.

Aboriginal Belief

All along patiently
we watched you take our land, forests and sky.
We stayed peaceful and composed and dispossessed.
We tolerated you rape our children and women
all night long, all night long.
We accepted the injustice in the name of your God,
civility, benevolence and humility.
We smoked peace pipes and offered our love
to no avail.
We kept dreaming and baking bread
tiling the land and harvesting the crops.
To forget our dreams we turned to alcohol
to kill our hopes of beautiful dawn.
Homeless we became in our own homes.
We cry inside and do not laugh, though you
may not believe. When will this all end
we do not know but we welcome
you may come and go.
We share this vast bounty of ours and
wish you well.

Who are you?

Shake my sleep
Tugging my heart stings

Making me dream
Calling my name
Pulling me magnetic
Electrifying my senses

Making me hum with joy
Sigh with sorrow
Light my darkness
Disappear

You Can Too

I am in you and you are in me.
I am here and there, both ever and never.
You are now and eternity, continuity of a flow.
I am a moon and you a dreamer.
You complement me and I complete you.
We are just two halves of ONE.

It's the beauty of our hearts, depth of our souls,
kindness of actions, capacity to love,
ability to forgive, and knack to appreciate,
absorb, and express that make us human.

I sow seeds of dreams
and wait for them to sprout
but I am not the soil
nor I am the water.

You too can grow
what you want.

Caroline 'Ceri Naz' Nazareno

Carolin 'Ceri' Nazareno

Caroline Nazareno-Gabis a.k.a. Ceri Naz, born in Anda, Pangasinan known as a 'poet of peace and friendship', is a multi-awarded poet, journalist, editor, publicist, linguist, educator, and women's advocate.

Graduated cum laude with the degree of Bachelor of Elementary Education, specialized in General Science at Pangasinan State University. Ceri have been a voracious researcher in various arts, science and literature. She volunteered in Richmond Multicultural Concerns Society, TELUS World Science, Vancouver Art Gallery, and Vancouver Aquarium.

She was privileged to be chosen as one of the Directors of Writers Capital International Foundation (WCIF), Member of the Poetry Posse, one of the Board of Directors of Galaktika ATUNIS Magazine based in Albania; the World Poetry Canada and International Director to Philippines; Global Citizen's Initiatives Member, Association for Women's rights in Development (AWID) and Anacbanua. She has been a 4th Placer in World Union of Poets Poetry Prize 2016, Writers International Network-Canada ''Amazing Poet 2015'', The Frang Bardhi Literary Prize 2014 (Albania), the sair-gazeteci or Poet-Journalist Award 2014 (Tuzla, Istanbul, Turkey) and World Poetry Empowered Poet 2013 (Vancouver, Canada).

Dreamcatcher

Weave the web
let your bad dreams fade
In a web-like scenario
Fancied with yarns, beads, and feathers
Inside the sacred hoop,
Someone's calling
To escape nightmares

Hang the catcher
let the legends punch
move in circles
chime in the wind
and fly in
the wings of sweetdreams.

Native Voices

Across the regions
Home of ruling families
Under the earth-berm dwellings
Walled with ritual contexts

Tribal drums, echoing horns
Call for a flight
Or fight for the oases
A never fallen legacy
Language of diversity.

Carolin 'Ceri' Nazareno

Street Mumbles

I am anonymous
considered preterit forms-
every detail of cars,
daily rates in hostels,
99-cents shampoo,
Picco's thin crust pizza and
homemade gelato
while I pinned maps
at Boston streets

I learned a little Irish song at a tea party
sat a little while, juggled words of wisdom
as if I knew the revolution in Worcester
tried to wipe every brewed coffee drops
from my Chelsea boots and leather jacket

I rested my back and stammered
whisked the smokes I breathe
from the other table, reminded me
of a certain voice. I chuckled,
there was another castle in the air
in a pool of memories.

Swapna Behera

Swapna Behera is a bilingual contemporary poet, author, translator and editor from Odisha, India .She was a teacher from 1984 to 2015 . Her stories, poems and articles are widely published in National and International journals, and ezines, and are translated into different national and International languages. She has penned four books. She was conferred upon the Prestigious International Poesis Award of Honor at the 2nd Bharat Award for Literature as Jury in 2015, The Enchanting Muse Award in India World Poetree Festival 2017, World Icon of Peace Award in 2017, and the Pentasi B World Fellow Poet in 2017.. She is the recipient of Gold Cross Of Wisdom Award ,the medal for The Best Teachers of the World from World Union of Poets in 2018, and The LIfe time Achievement Award ,The Best Planner Award, The Sahitya Shiromani Award, ATAL BiHARI BAJPAYEE AWARD 2018, Ambassador De Literature Award 2018 .She is the Ambassador of Humanity by Hafrikan Prince Art World Africa 2018 and an official member of World Nation's Writers Union ,Kazakhstan2018. At present she is the manager at Large, Planner and Columnist of The Literati, the administrator of several poetic groups ,the member of the Special Council of Five of World Union of Poets and the Cultural Ambassador of Inner Child Press U.S.

Someone Hides Under The Ground

Someone hides under the ground
May be the blood of our ancestors
Their stoic silence hoots the glory
The corn trees manifest the secret diary

Someone hides beyond the clouds
May be a sensible thinker shines
The eyes had to go through the tears
To see the rainbows
Rocks of Peru crush for new soil
As everyday a new prayer traipses
The hilly hamlet sings the hymn

Someone hides in the wood
May be the moon sprints
And texts are predefined
To save the last breathe of nature

Magnitude - -

Ask a soldier
the magnitude of the vow
His wife's broken bangles will reply

Ask the waiter in the Restaurant
The magnitude of poverty
The scar on his cheek will reply

Ask the farmer in the field
The magnitude of profit and loss
His rotten tomatoes will reply

Ask the single mother
The magnitude of solitude
Sweating of her forehead will reply

Ask the paper note
The magnitude of Price Index
It will hop thousand hands with joy

Ask the life
The magnitude of love
The death will reply - - - -

Don't Ever ---

Don't ever talk so much
Words will inscribe
In the ether
History will witness
The depth. height and weight of your words
do they carry
empathy, blessings or pride ??

Don't ever talk so much
On every street the bubble
of your words
Words are smokes
Rising from the rice pots
Or of the pyre

Don't ever talk so much
Till now tears of maps
on grim faces
words are vapours or volcanoes
pearls or papers
or entwined waves
words are trump cards of your logics
or of your stump card !!!!
Don't ever talk so much ------

-

......

William S. Peters Sr.

Bill's writing career spans a period of over 50 years. Being first Published in 1972, Bill has since went on to Author in excess of 40 additional Volumes of Poetry, Short Stories, etc., expressing his thoughts on matters of the Heart, Spirit, Consciousness and Humanity. His primary focus is that of Love, Peace and Understanding!

Bill says . . .

I have always likened Life to that of a Garden. So, for me, Life is simply about the Seeds we Sow and Nourish. All things we "Think and Do", will "Be" Cause and eventually manifest itself to being an "Effect" within our own personal "Existences" and "Experiences" . . . whether it be Fruit, Flowers, Weeds or Barren Landscapes! Bill highly regards the Fruits of his Labor and wishes that everyone would thus go on to plant "Lovely" Seeds on "Good Ground" in their own Gardens of Life!

to connect with Bill, he is all things Inner Child

www.iaminnerchild.com

Personal Web Site

www.iamjustbill.com

We shall pray

Perhaps it is a fear
That prevails,
Within you,
The uncertainty
Of the unknown
That gave cause for your dismissal
Of we the people
Of the land,
The rivers,
The mountains,
The sky
And that of all life

We are indigenous

You can not steal our history,
But your lies,
Your forked tongue
Prevent a true 'knowing'

It did not stop you
From the carnage
You wreaked
Upon our people
And that of creation

Your greed to possess
That which you never can
Drove you westward
Polluting the landscapes
As you journeyed,
And still

There is not enough
For you

We have been tolerant,
We have embraced your young zeal,
But your roots are not here,
Yet you claim
ALL
As your own

You store curses upon yourselves
In the darkened closets of your hearts
And you dare speak of 'light'

Look about you 'settler'
We are all brothers
And sisters . . .

Until you realize
This simple truth
Suffering will walk with you
Every step
Of your way

When will you ever learn ?

We shall pray for your awakening

Discovery

She brought out my magnificence
As I attempted
To bring hers about
As well

We felt compelled
To share this gift
Of each other
With the world

We journeyed
We met many souls
Who beheld us
Where we are beholding . . .
In our hearts

Yes, we love each other
And our sisters and brothers
As well

From land to land
And back to our homestand
We saw the sights,
The lights . . .
By day
And by night

We were embraced
By cultures discovered
Uncovered
By the lovers
Of life

Yes, there was strife
But that did not stop
The children
From smiling . . .
And adults as well

I can not begin to tell you
About all
That we discovered . . .
uncovered

We were witnesses
To the greater aspects
Of what humanity is,
Can be,
And is becoming

And all of this
Is . . . simply
Because
We danced
In our hearts
As we were enhanced
As we strove
To discover our
Magnificence
And your as well

Discovery

Can you hear it ? . . .

The BIG GUYS
Who ruled the world
Did not even know
That they existed . . .
Nor did they care

So many of their family members,
Friends and neighbors
Have departed
To other lands
Or to heaven

The noise of the bombs
And the hungry bellies
Roared in a dis-harmonic un-symphonic way
But not one of the BIG GUYS
Could heard the music
For they were marching
To the beat of a soulless drum

Can you hear it ? . . .

January 2019

Features

~ * ~

Houda Elfchtali

Anthony 'Endurer' Briscoe

Iram Fatima 'Ashi'

Dr. K. K. Mathew

i Fly

because I Can

...said the Dreamer to the world.

www.iamjustbill.com

94

Houda
Elfchtali

Houda Elfchtali

Houda Elfchtali hails from Morocco

Teacher of English in Morocco

President of the section of Meknes of the league of Moroccan Writers

Delegate in Meknes of "100 thousand poets for change" of " Motivatiomal Strips" and of " Afropoesie"

Literary Consultant in the Forum of Poetry in India

Author of " My words and Worlds" and " " Shades of my soul"

Vice president of association" 8 Mars de la peche no kill et de la preservation de la nature"

Vice president in in the association "Meknes Chorus"

Member singer alto in Meknes Chorus

Viennese Waltz
A tribute to A.Mozart and A.Renoir

My heart is
Full of
Some Weirdest
kinds of love ...
It can thus ..
Caress the word
And tell its softness
Smell the sound
And sing its fragrance
View the silence
swim in its vibes
And dream its colours
Climb the skies
Feel their heights
And dance
With its orbits
Approach the stars
Touch their texture
And poetise
Their glitter
Hug the trees
And bless the earth
For their greens
Melt with rivers
And slightly flow
Like tiny waves
in their beds
Gaze at the sun
grasp its rays
And kiss their ligh
Venerate the rain

And make an orchestra
Where my soul
is maestro
And where the Universe
Plays Mozart
And talently dances
Viennese Waltzes

I Am That One ..

I am that walker ..
That would step
in the sand
And leave prints on it
Of my history
And of all the shapes
That life painted
On the surface
Of my being
I am that talker ..
That would opt
For silence
To tell the story
That paints the cores
Of humanity
And seek
for distant shores
To send messages
That would be received
With wisdom and love
And with the truest
Sensations
I am that dreamer ..
That would close my eyes
To seek the plain truth
That my unconsciousness
Might reveal
And then open them
And still keep dreaming
Of sunny winters
Snowy summers
And lost springs

I am that lover
That would talk
to your eyes
Listen to the music
Of your unheard strings
And feel the warmth
Of your skin
From the tender vibes
Of your uncommon voice
I m that singer
That the mermaids envy
In the deepest waters
Where the tiniest creatures
Sing and dance
To the bluest ocean s
Water made sounds

The Thinker
A tribute to Franz Kafka and Virginia Woolf

..And you keep thinking
And thinking it over
Analysing
the whos and whys
Questionning
The crucial evidence
..You keep wondering
Why and what ..
And it grows ..
High in your mind
It crawls through you ..
Like a snake in the desert
It crosses ..
your tiniest veins
And gets to your heart ..
It shapes the core ..
Of your conception
It grasps the fragments ..
Of your perception
Torments your soul ..
Tears it apart
And it s exhausting
It makes you run
in your place
And Fly
into the depths
Of your destiny ..
It makes you sink
In oceans of the self ..
And dive..
In streams

Of your consciousness
Like in "Virginia Woolf" s art
Confusion it is
Everywhere in you
Even in the air
You breathe..
In your hair..
You can feel it act
And under your skin
It reacts ..
And then
You realize
That deep inside
You are not you
You are thought and chaos ..
You are floods , seisms
A tsunami of words
That hit and knock
Into your brain
Making it restless
Captured inside
And capturing you
Not allowing
the least of you
To come to peace

Houda Elfchtali

Athony 'Endurer' Briscoe

Anthony Briscoe is a spoken word/hip hop artist from Chicago. He has a style of poetry and music that infuses a plethora of life experiences to reach the young people in the City of Chicago. He is a veteran of the United States Armed Forces, an ordained minister, and sits on the Board of the Brazier Veteran's Resource Center.

He is a motivational speaker and has addressed youth in small and large group settings throughout the Chicagoland area. His passion and creative methods of urging youth to rise above their circumstances and champion success is also felt in his work as a technologist. He is a published devotional writer for the Apostolic Church of God and his poetry is featured in the award winning spoken word group People of Extraordinary Talent. He has spoken publicly for corporations like the Jack & Jill Foundation, Chicago Public Schools, CHAMPS Male Mentoring Program, Boeing International and the Noble Network of Charter Schools. This Chicago native also released his debut hip hop album, My Journey, in September of 2018.

Somber

He is awake, paralyzed by stagnation
Wanting to wake up and live his dream
But it's not visible, tangible, no manifestation
Life, just dreary and slowly crawling

It's late, pouring hours into a job that has left him lifeless
Barren, friendless, visionless, hopeless
He sees the reflection in the mirror, and it is not his
It's a former life, of great faith and trust in the Lord

He smiles for a moment and thinks of a guy he once knew
A dreamer, hopeful, youthful, ready to take on the world
He misses that man and wishes he would once again visit
with him
Tell him that he still believes he can dream, hope, trust,
build

Scantily rhythms run syncopated over hollow shadows
Cracked surfaces pray for a little bit of rain so they can feel
healed
Breathe, sing, before the sun scorches away that drop of
sweetness
Leaving them dry, corroded, shattered, frozen

For a minute, he envisions being in that special place
His passion, his calling, his life, his lung
But it's late and before he finds rest, the alarm clock sounds
Five years in, dreams forgotten, hope deferred has made his
heart sick
He celebrates that life of joy his friends have that have
taken that leap of faith
A report is due, he punches the clock, drinks the coffee of
routine
Eats at the table of hesitation, and sees an RSS feed of his
favorite Poet….that could have been me…..

The Toils of War

My body came back whole
But my mind came back cold
Like the steel in my hand massaging triggers
At unseen enemies moving through Vietcong jungles
Trip wires under my feet, ringing ears flat on my back
Unable to move, America this is not your war
But I'm here and I want to go back home to my family
At home high school over, college bound, mom crying with
a letter in hand
You've been drafted, dreams shattered
Fear gripping my throat wondering if I'll see her again
These trees move fast, impossible to chase these ghosts
That dance with angels after blowing themselves up
But my fallen brothers dance, lying in paths of blood
Lining the Ho Chi Man Trail
No niggas, no crackers, no wetbacks, no spics, no wasp

It took the death of a unit to find out the only color we hand
it common was red
With vengeance and anger and rage and pain we swoop
down
Like silent hornets on a village of women washing clothes
and kids playing
They never knew what hit them and we never knew what
possessed us
Deafened by the screams of a foreign language
No doubt from the violent rupturing of her vagina
Or, maybe from watching her child's neck being snapped
like a twig
The aroma of death is merciless and I wreak
Vengeance is not a dish best served cold but one left to the
gods

Anthony 'Endurer' Briscoe

Smoke burns for hours and we all stand there
Unphased because satan has made us callous
No more screams, the trees have stopped moving
We stare at 37 bodies whose death did not bring back our
brothers
Realizing that they bleed like we do
64 years old, I stare at this wall of history and all the lives
lost
But it's missing 37 names
Whose voices haunt me daily
Whose faces cry me to sleep
They too were red

Trafficked

Memories, like the corners of her mine

When she was 6 years old she had a dream
Being tickled awake, hidden under her bedroom sheets, and
a voice that melted her heart, screamed, "Wake up Baby
Girl Wake up"
And she would scream out in laughter
"Dad stop, I'm up, stop, I'm up" and they would say
morning prayers together
Open her bedroom curtains
On the days it was raining they would race with raindrops
on windows pane
And on the days it was bright they would blow kisses to the
sun
And let its rays grace their face with sheer warmth, they
were close
Could it be that it was all so simple then?
Is it but a dream or could it be reality?

Memories, like the corners of his mind

When he was 49 he dreamed of her graduation
Walking across the stage in flats because she hated hills
Beauty and as charming as her mother, she made him proud
Made him feel like a Father and for all the mistakes he
made
He watched her walk with grace and elegance and thought
to himself, I got something right
I did one thing good, I raised a history maker
But he knew even in his dream, she saved him more than
he could ever save her
His earthly angel becoming a woman
Has time rewritten every line?
If we only had a chance to do it all again.

Memories, like the corners of their mind

Stomach queasy, 20 years on the force and his heart is
broken
An 18 hour shift comes to an end, 8 AM he walks into the
house
He falls in his wife's arms and cries
She was in tears long before he came home when she saw
him on the 6 o'clock news
16 year old girl missing 2 months body found mutilated,
unrecognizable.
Their baby, their angel, fruit of her womb, jewel of his
loins
Strayed once to a party with a friend she met on snapchat
and it was her last
She made the news and history at the same time

Misty watered shattered memories of the way they were

For almost 20 years married men, took fellas only trips to
Brazil while their wives turned their heads
Silence is as complicit as intention
Not to mention these girls and women they were going to
see where under the worse conditions
See what would happen if men started looking at all young
girls as their daughters and not a prize
What if men starting seeing hearts and not thighs
Oh how we have turned on those who gave us life
With the promise of money or the threat of a knife

96% of women and girls exploited across the planet and
we give them iPhone
2 Million children underage with social media accounts and
we give them the internet
Young girl molested in a video shopped around on
Facebook and all were enraged
But Facebook protest are as useless as twits who tweet

You're trying to see who like your post
Probably just a many of our daughters that went missing
worldwide this week

Social media has become the new window to the world
And online BFF's has become the death and kidnapping of
girls
ROBLOX and Minecraft chats rooms
Seducing our children into taking pictures of themselves
It's a dangerous ground when they get value from someone
else
While politicians who passed laws, in the dark corners of
the web
Log into their accounts because private servers tell no
secrets

We are at war, militaries take countries
We just want them to take our daughters away from
suffering and bring them home
Parents, trust but verify
Pastor's Extend
Rabbi's Mobilize
Imam's Collaborate
Citizens, be humane

Sex trafficking, $99 billion dollar a year business this is a
worldwide situation
2 million children exploited every year in the sex trade,
someone tell me the state of our United Nation

Do something!

Anthony 'Endurer' Briscoe

Iram
Fatima
'Ashi'

I am Iram Fatima 'Ashi'. I am nonresident Indian staying in Saudi Arabia. I have lived in different places and explored different people and their cultures. I am connected with my own country by soul and miss that.

Travelling has been an important part of my life. I have always felt as though borders are just the constructs of our feeble intellects, we have to look beyond them, only then will our hearts be free. *After spending so many years in different cultures and places, my quest is far from over. I have accepted whole world as my own and have a deep desire to be buried wherever I die.*

I like reading, writing, painting, listening to music and observing nature. I take inspiration from real life, nature and anything which touches me. I am part of 44 books and winner of 3 awards from Aagman for my literary contribution, I am a poetess, writer, painter and overall an artist by heart.

Happy Reading...
Love
Iram Fatima 'Ashi'

Desired Dream

Start the story from where we had left, build a bridge from
past to present,
Lying together, holding hands, listening songs of each
other's choice,
Getting cozy and showering kisses as we never had before,
Is this the deep desired dream, that I lived with you in my
real life?

A hunger of love was there, the longing thirst was over
powering,
A wish for togetherness was hunting our inner loving
being,
You and me were alone since centuries, lived life in
moments,
Is this the deep desired dream, that I lived with you in my
real life?

A joy that transferred soul to soul through worldly bodies,
A touch of each other that filled with gratification for two
individuals,
Left an entire universe behind while peeking into each
other's eyes,
Is this the deep desired dream, that I lived with you in my
real life?

We accepted all our differences, the cracks of past which
was between us,
You poured your affection and cured the deep scars of my
body and soul,
You gave life to my living body and reason to be happy till
last,
Is this the deep desired dream, that I lived with you in my
real life?

I Choose You

Everyone's desires don't get fulfilled,
Your wants are sometimes, beyond your skill,
You don't do things according to your will,
But I choose you, out of odds for me...

In the journey, people come and go with time,
There are always the Rocky Mountains to climb,
Life is not a poem with perfect rhyme,
But I choose you, out of odds for me...

We were opposite and disagreed with each other,
Strangers for each and unacceptable rather,
Nature secretly arranged our gather,
But I choose you, out of odds for me...

A strange sentiment was felt by both,
We went through an emotional growth,
Now it's time for promises and oath,
But I choose you, out of odds for me...

Now you become confused,
And it's time to separate and lose,
I moved by making you my muse,
And I choose you, out of odds for me.

Beginning

The first cry after birth, a beginning towards life,
The first fall after crawl, you stand up and walk,
A push from behind, to make you run fast,
Is the sign of beginning and inspiration to move on.

A betrayal from loved one, a realization of relationships,
An enemy who hurts, a support of loving friends,
A failure of hard work, an added craving for lost goal,
Is the sign of beginning and inspiration to move on.

Set your aim of life and rush to get your purpose,
Life is not an achievement it is a learning process,
A journey that makes you travel and takes you for a toss,
Is the sign of beginning and inspiration to move on.

Dr. K. K. Mathew

Dr. K. K. Mathew

Dr.K.K.Mathew is a reputed physician and medical scientist of international repute. He has done many innovations in medical science and some are the first of its kind. He is reputed poet and novelist. He has written nine collection of poems.

Tone of Love

The love immortal decays today like hard mass,
delicate filamentous one turns rough solidness
the love now cannot fly, it stays on earth as it
is like the heavy material that bears gravity, if
thrown up comes down as it carries mass, the
one without body doesn't come down if thrown
up as it is very delicate filamentous fused with
the soul that too doesn't bear any weight, both
fly to the horizon of tranquility and to the infinity
while the one with gravity, the materialistic, stays
on land, decays and even putrefies and dissolve in
soil; the delicate fused one lives ever, flies to infinity.

Eternal Peace

The one, man aspires for, the world craves for,
the one before you like a mirage, the moment
you reach it, it escapes by a whisker, the greatest
gift by God was spoiled by the misdeed of man.
the world is turbulent, highly inflammable, might
explode any moment, peace is miles and miles
away, it is a dream only; it cannot be bought by
money as it comes spontaneously in the mind.
when God enters heart, the passion all vanish,
a new dawn begins, a heart without excessive
passion for the world and worldly, as God wipes
out all dirt, washes heart with divinity, heart becomes
pure and holy and it is filled with eternal peace.

Dr. K. K. Mathew

The Beauty of Beauty

What is it, beauty of beauty, is it the beauty extreme
how is it, how to identify it, is it detected with naked
eyes, is there any limit to it; it is something beyond,
the words cannot describe it, it cannot be detected
with the external senses, the whole concept of beauty
changed when the actual perception comes, the
interior beauty is grasped with the opened internal sense.
it much more accentuated and magnified, that the
external senses cannot grasp it, the perception of
divinity with the opened internal sense, it is the beauty
with extreme purity which the naked eyes cannot detect.

Remembering

our fallen soldiers of verse

Janet Perkins Caldwell

February 14, 1959 ~ September 20, 2016

Alan W. Jankowski

16 March 1961 ~ 10 March 2017

Dr. K. K. Mathew

Inner Child Press

News

We are so excited to announce the New and upcoming books of some of our Poetry Posse authors.

On the following pages we present to you ...

Jackie Davis Allen

Gail Weston Shazor

hülya n. yılmaz

Nizar Sartawi

Faleeha Hassan

Caroline 'Ceri' Nazareno

William S. Peters, Sr.

Now Available at
www.innerchildpress.com

No Illusions

Through the Looking Glass

Jackie Davis Allen

Now Available at
www.innerchildpress.com

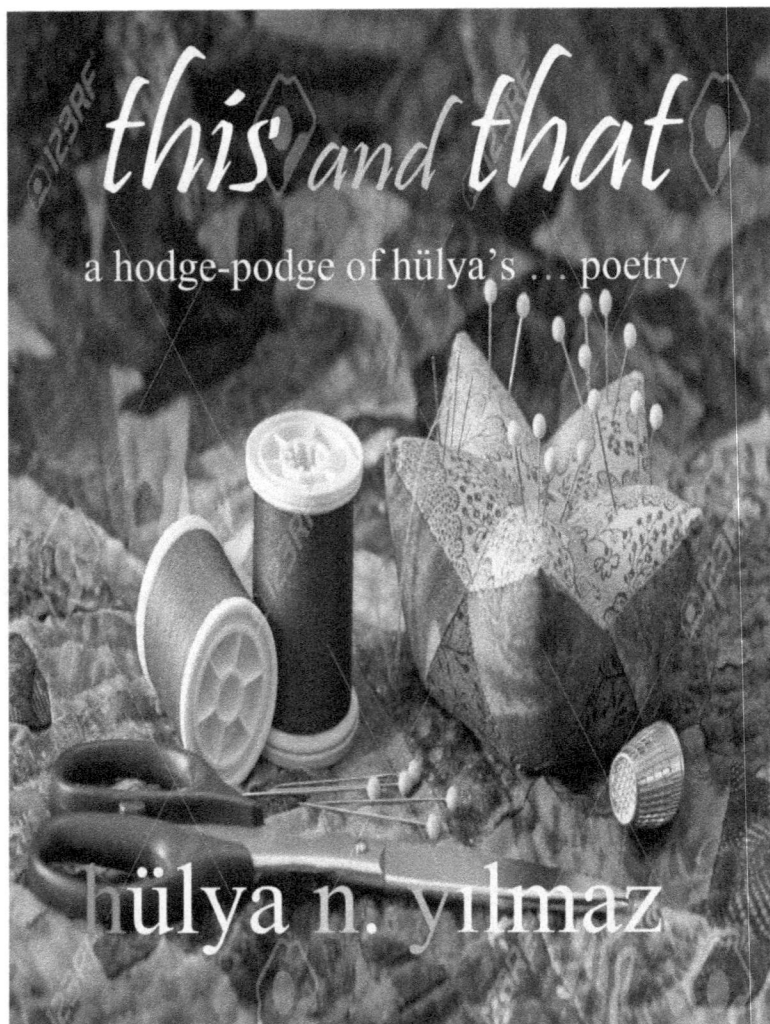

this and that
a hodge-podge of hülya's ... poetry

hülya n. yılmaz

Now Available at

www.innerchildpress.com

Jackie Davis Allen

Now Available at
www.innerchildpress.com

Lies
My
Grandfathers
Told
Me

Gail Weston Shazor

Now Available at
www.innerchildpress.com

Aflame

Memoirs in Verse

hülya n. yılmaz

Now Available at
www.innerchildpress.com

Now Available at
www.innerchildpress.com

Inner Child Press News

Now Available at
www.innerchildpress.com

Breakfast

for

Butterflies

Faleeha Hassan

Now Available at
www.innerchildpress.com

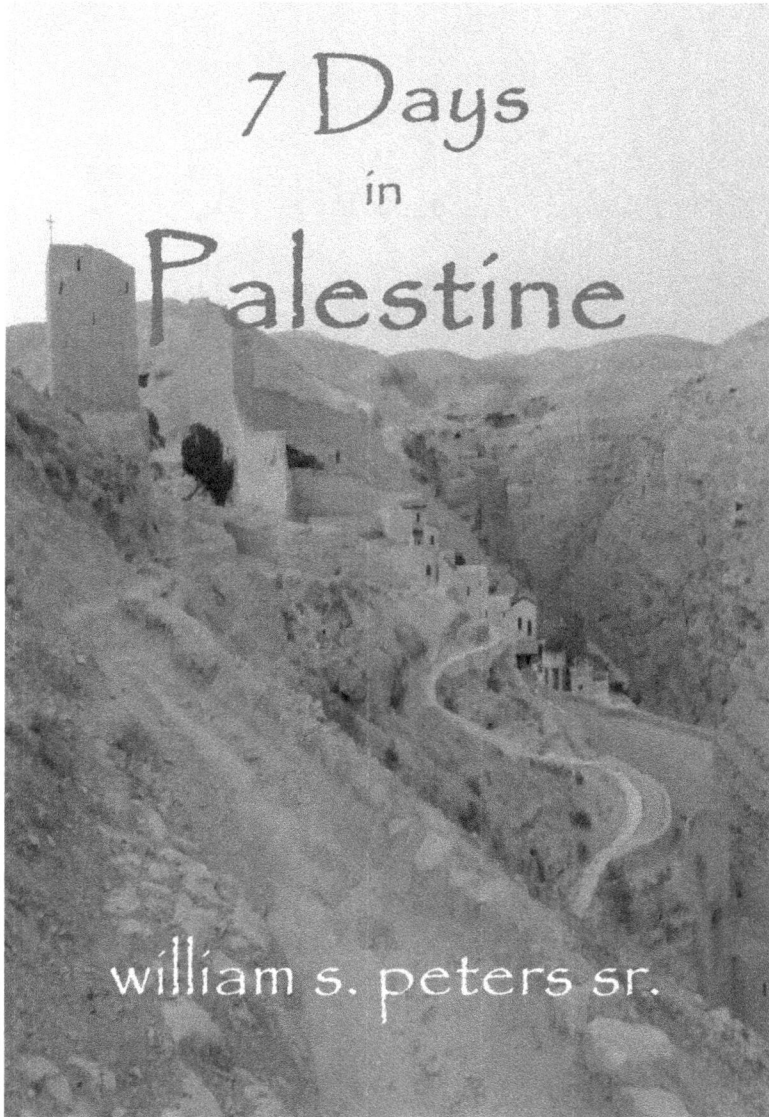

7 Days
in
Palestine

william s. peters sr.

Now Available at
www.innerchildpress.com

inner child press
presents

Tunisia My Love

william s. peters, sr.

Coming in Spring of 2019

eclectic verse

mommy i hear those whispers . . .
(again)

willIAM s. PeTers, sR.

Coming in Spring of 2019

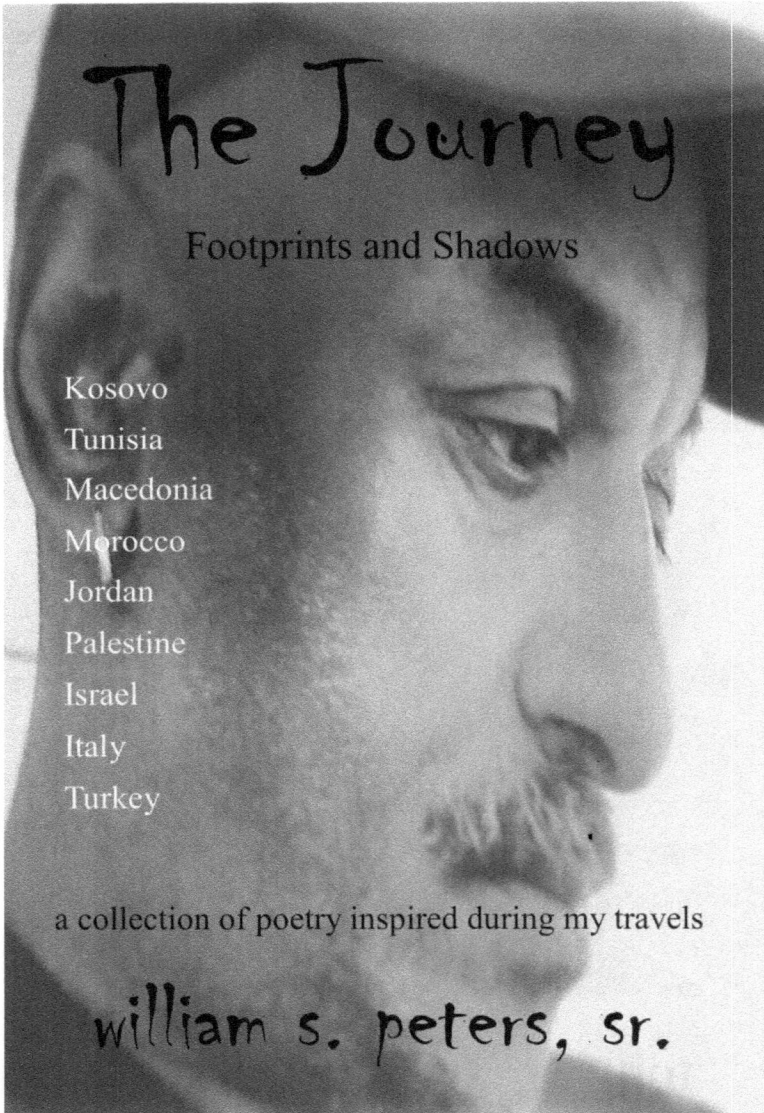

The Journey

Footprints and Shadows

Kosovo
Tunisia
Macedonia
Morocco
Jordan
Palestine
Israel
Italy
Turkey

a collection of poetry inspired during my travels

william s. peters, sr.

Now Available at
www.innerchildpress.com

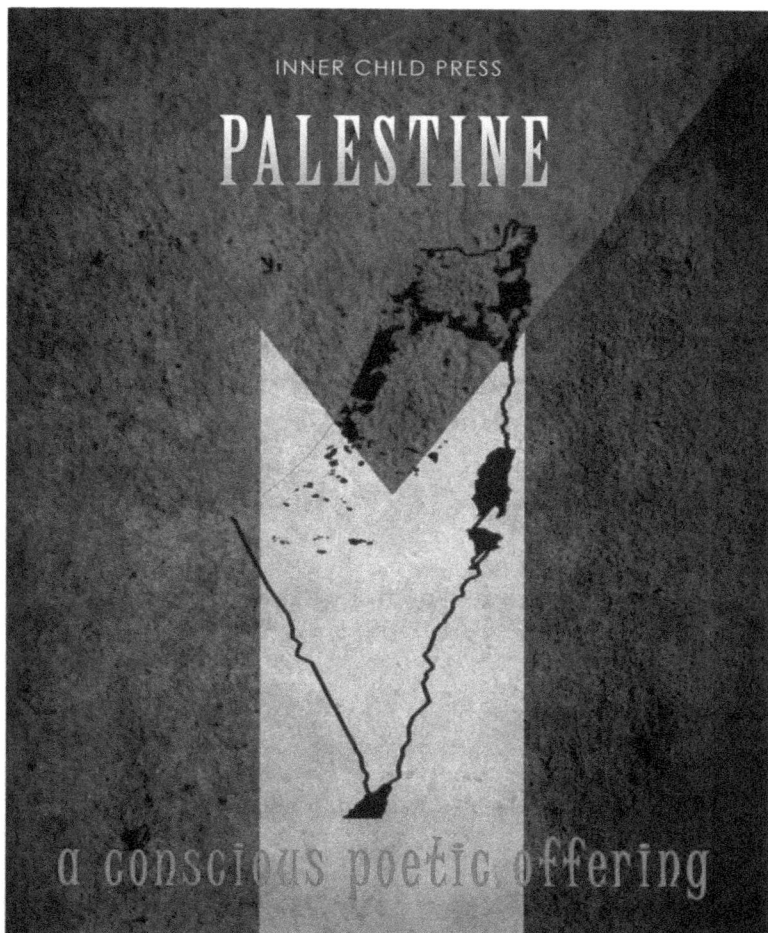

Now Available at
www.innerchildpress.com

Now Available at
www.innerchildpress.com

INNER CHILD PRESS

THIS IS WHY I
SLEEP

william s. peters sr.

Now Available at
www.innerchildpress.com

Inward Reflections

This could work...

Yes...

I got it...

Ohh...

Think on These Things
Book II

william s. peters, sr.

Now Available at
www.innerchildpress.com

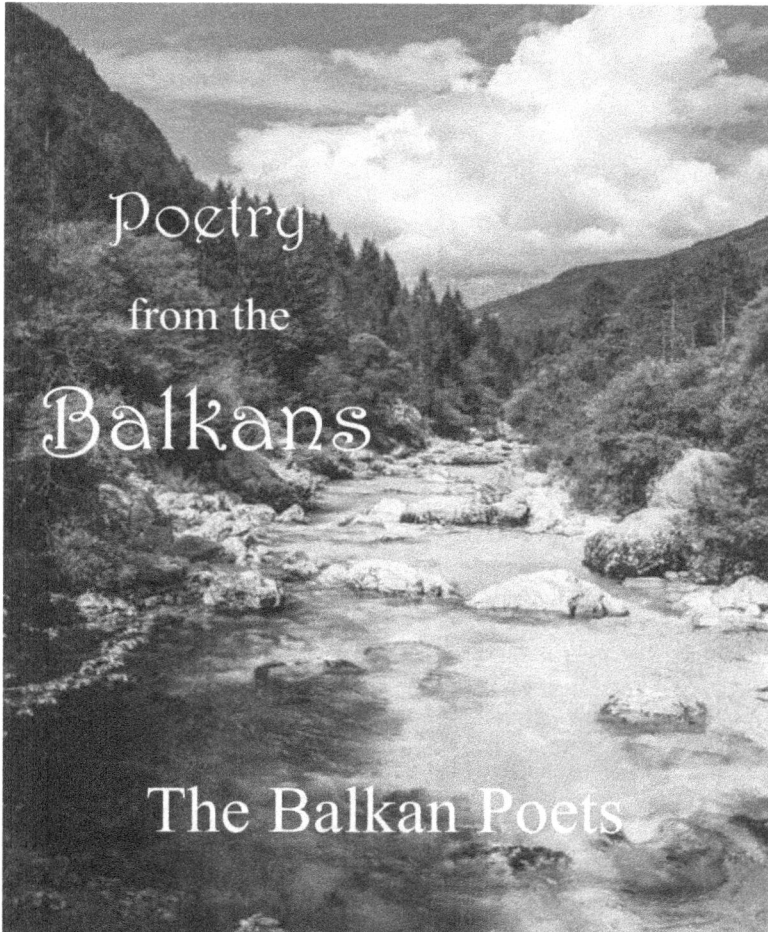

Other

Anthological

works from

Inner Child Press International

www.innerchildpress.com

Janet

gone too soon . . .

Now Available

www.innerchildpress.com/janet-p-caldwell.php

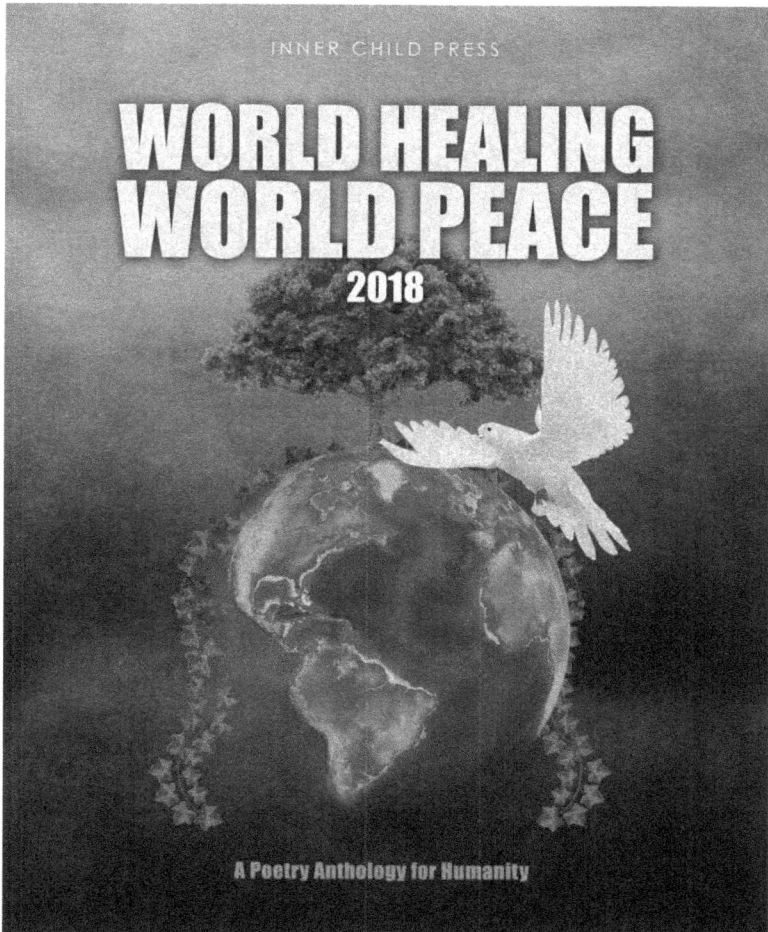

INNER CHILD PRESS

WORLD HEALING WORLD PEACE
2018

A Poetry Anthology for Humanity

Now Available

www.worldhealingworldpeacepoetry.com

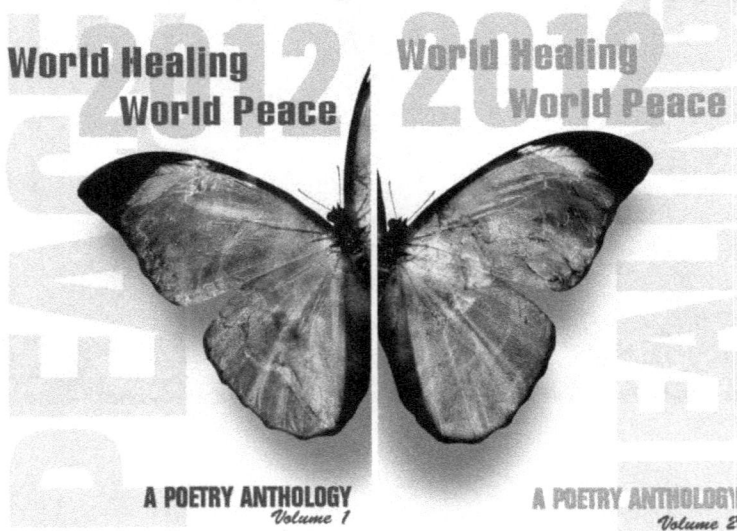

Now Available

www.worldhealingworldpeacepoetry.com

Now Available

www.innerchildpress.com/anthologies

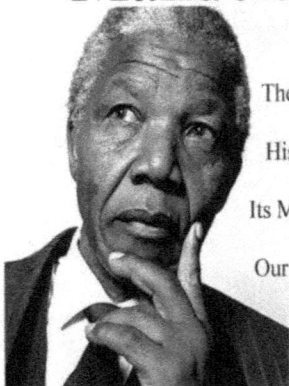

Inner Child Press Anthologies

Mandela

The Man

His Life

Its Meaning

Our Words

Poetry . . . Commentary & Stories
The Anthological Writers

A GATHERING OF WORDS

POETRY & COMMENTARY
FOR
TRAYVON MARTIN

INNER CHILD PRESS

BLACK MALE-D

The Black Male Writers
with words from Imam Jamil Abdullah Al-Amin
aka H. Rap Brown

I
want
my
poetry
to... volume 4

the conscious poets
inspired by ... Monte Smith

Now Available

www.innerchildpress.com/anthologies

Now Available

www.innerchildpress.com/anthologies

healing through words

Poetry ... Prose ... Prayer ... Stories

a
Poetically
Spoken
Anthology
volume I
Collector's Edition

The Poetry Posse
Presents

an anthology
of

Love

The Poetry Posse 2016

Now Available

www.innerchildpress.com/anthologies

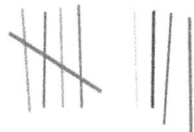

Now Available

www.innerchildpress.com/anthologies

The Year of the Poet
January 2014

The Poetry Posse

Jamie Bond
Gail Weston Shazor
Albert 'Infinite' Carrasco
Siddartha Beth Pierce
Janet P. Caldwell
June 'Bugg' Barefield
Debbie M. Allen
Tony Henninger
Joe DaVerbal Minddancer
Robert Gibbous
Neetu Wali
Shareef Abdur-Rasheed
William S. Peters, Sr.

Carnation

Our January Feature
Terri L. Johnson

the Year of the Poet
February 2014

violets

The Poetry Posse

Jamie Bond
Gail Weston Shazor
Albert 'infinite' Carrasco
Siddartha Beth Pierce
Janet P. Caldwell
June 'Bugg' Barefield
Debbie M. Allen
Tony Henninger
Joe DaVerbal Minddancer
Robert Gibbous
Neetu Wali
Shareef Abdur-Rasheed
William S. Peters, Sr.

Our February Features
Teresa E. Gallion & Robert Gibson

the Year of the Poet
March 2014

The Poetry Posse

Jamie Bond
Gail Weston Shazor
Albert 'Infinite' Carrasco
Siddartha Beth Pierce
Janet P. Caldwell
June 'Bugg' Barefield
Debbie M. Allen
Tony Henninger
Joe DaVerbal Minddancer
Robert Gibbous
Neetu Wali
Kimberly Burnham
William S. Peters, Sr.

daffodil

Our March Featured Poets
Alicia C. Cooper & hülya yılmaz

the Year of the Poet
April 2014

The Poetry Posse

Jamie Bond
Gail Weston Shazor
Albert 'Infinite' Carrasco
Siddartha Beth Pierce
Janet P. Caldwell
June 'Bugg' Barefield
Debbie M. Allen
Tony Henninger
Joe DaVerbal Minddancer
Robert Gibbous
Neetu Wali
Shareef Abdur-Rasheed
Kimberly Burnham
William S. Peters, Sr.

Our April Featured Poets
Fahredin Shehu
Martina Reisz Newberry
Justin Blackburn
Monte Smith

Sweet Pea

celebrating international poetry month

Now Available

www.innerchildpress.com/the-year-of-the-poet

the year of the poet
May 2014

May's Featured Poets

ReeCee
Joski the Poet
Shannon Stanton

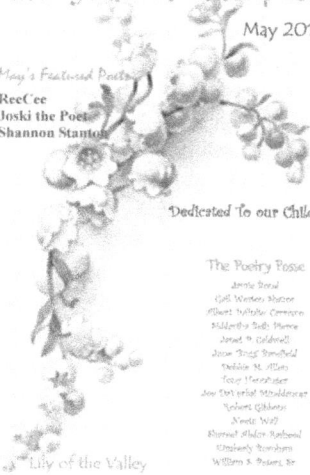

Dedicated to our Children

The Poetry Posse

Jamie Bond
Gail Weston Shazor
Albert Infinite Carrasco
Siddartha Beth Pierce
Janet P. Caldwell
Jackie Tragg Bransfield
Debbie M. Allen
Tony Henninger
Joe DeVerbal Minddancer
Robert Gibbons
Neetu Wali
Shareef Abdur-Rasheed
Kimberly Burnham
William S. Peters, Sr.

Lily of the Valley

the Year of the Poet
June 2014

Love & Relationship

Rose

June's Featured Poets

Shantelle McLin
Jacqueline D. E. Kennedy
Abraham N. Benjamin

The Poetry Posse

Jamie Bond
Gail Weston Shazor
Albert Infinite Carrasco
Siddartha Beth Pierce
Janet P. Caldwell
Jackie Bugg Bransfield
Debbie M. Allen
Tony Henninger
Joe DeVerbal Minddancer
Robert Gibbons
Neetu Wali
Shareef Abdur-Rasheed
Kimberly Burnham
William S. Peters, Sr.

The Year of the Poet
July 2014

July Feature Poets

Christena A. V. Williams
Dr. John R. Strum
Kolade OlanrewaSu Freedom

The Poetry Posse

Jamie Bond
Gail Weston Shazor
Albert Infinite Carrasco
Siddartha Beth Pierce
Janet P. Caldwell
Jackie Bugg Bransfield
Debbie M. Allen
Tony Henninger
Joe DeVerbal Minddancer
Robert Gibbons
Neetu Wali
Shareef Abdur-Rasheed
Kimberly Burnham
William S. Peters, Sr.

Lotus
Asian Flower of the Month

The Year of the Poet
August 2014

Gladiolus

The Poetry Posse

Jamie Bond
Gail Weston Shazor
Albert Infinite Carrasco
Siddartha Beth Pierce
Janet P. Caldwell
Jackie Bugg Bransfield
Debbie M. Allen
Tony Henninger
Joe DeVerbal Minddancer
Robert Gibbons
Neetu Wali
Shareef Abdur-Rasheed
Kimberly Burnham
William S. Peters, Sr.

August Feature Poets

Ann White * Rosalind Cherry * Sheila Jenkins

Now Available

www.innerchildpress.com/the-year-of-the-poet

159

The Year of the Poet
September 2014

Aster   Morning-Glory

Wild Garden of September Birth of Flower

September Feature Poets
Florence Malone * Keith Alan Hamilton

The Poetry Posse
Jamie Bond * Gail Weston Shazor * Albert 'Infinite' Carrasco * Siddartha Beth Pierce
Janet P. Caldwell * June 'Bugg' Barefield * Debbie M. Allen * Tony Henninger
Joe DaVerbal Minddancer * Robert Gibbons * Neetu Wali * Shareef Abdur-Rasheed
Kimberly Burnham * William S. Peters, Sr.

THE YEAR OF THE POET
October 2014

Red Poppy

The Poetry Posse
Jamie Bond * Gail Weston Shazor * Albert 'Infinite' Carrasco * Siddartha Beth Pierce
Janet P. Caldwell * June 'Bugg' Barefield * Debbie M. Allen * Tony Henninger
Joe DaVerbal Minddancer * Robert Gibbons * Neetu Wali * Shareef Abdur-Rasheed
Kimberly Burnham * William S. Peters, Sr.

October Feature Poets
Ceri Naz * RaJendra Padhi * Elizabeth Castillo

THE YEAR OF THE POET
November 2014

Chrysanthemum

The Poetry Posse
Jamie Bond * Gail Weston Shazor * Albert 'Infinite' Carrasco * Siddartha Beth Pierce
Janet P. Caldwell * June 'Bugg' Barefield * Debbie M. Allen * Tony Henninger
Joe DaVerbal Minddancer * Robert Gibbons * Neetu Wali * Shareef Abdur-Rasheed
Kimberly Burnham * William S. Peters, Sr.

November Feature Poets
Jocelyn Mosman * Jackie Allen * James Moore * Neville Hiatt

THE YEAR OF THE POET
December 2014

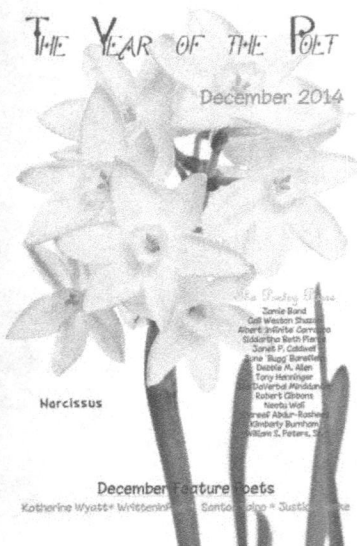

Narcissus

The Poetry Posse
Jamie Bond
Gail Weston Shazor
Albert Infinite Carrasco
Siddartha Beth Pierce
Janet P. Caldwell
June 'Bugg' Barefield
Debbie M. Allen
Tony Henninger
DaVerbal Minddancer
Robert Gibbons
Neetu Wali
Shareef Abdur-Rasheed
Kimberly Burnham
William S. Peters, Sr.

December Feature Poets
Katherine Wyatt* Wittenkindt * Santos Volpe * Justin Blake

Now Available

www.innerchildpress.com/the-year-of-the-poet

THE YEAR OF THE POET II
January 2015

Garnet

The Poetry Posse
Jamie Bond
Gail Weston Shazor
Albert 'Infinite' Carrasco
Siddartha Beth Pierce
Janet P. Caldwell
Tony Henninger
Joe DaVerbal Minddancer
Robert Gibbons
Neetu Wali
Shareef Abdur – Rasheed
Kimberly Burnham
Ann White
Keith Alan Hamilton
Katherine Wyatt
Fahredin Shehu
Hülya N. Yılmaz
Teresa E. Gallion
Jackie Allen
William S. Peters, Sr.

January Feature Poets
Bismay Mohanti * Jen Walls * Eric Judah

THE YEAR OF THE POET II
February 2015

Amethyst

THE POETRY POSSE
Jamie Bond
Gail Weston Shazor
Albert 'Infinite' Carrasco
Siddartha Beth Pierce
Janet P. Caldwell
Tony Henninger
Joe DaVerbal Minddancer
Robert Gibbons
Neetu Wali
Shareef Abdur – Rasheed
Kimberly Burnham
Ann White
Keith Alan Hamilton
Katherine Wyatt
Fahredin Shehu
Hülya N. Yılmaz
Teresa E. Gallion
Jackie Allen
William S. Peters, Sr.

FEBRUARY FEATURE POETS
Iram Fatima * Bob McNeil * Kerstin Centervall

The Year of the Poet II
March 2015

Our Featured Poets

Heung Sook * Anthony Arnold * Alicia Poland

Bloodstone

The Poetry Posse 2015
Jamie Bond * Gail Weston Shazor * Albert 'Infinite' Carrasco
Siddartha Beth Pierce * Janet P. Caldwell * Tony Henninger
Joe DaVerbal Minddancer * Neetu Wali * Shareef Abdur – Rasheed
Kimberly Burnham * Ann White * Keith Alan Hamilton
Katherine Wyatt * Fahredin Shehu * Hülya N. Yılmaz
Teresa E. Gallion * Jackie Allen * William S. Peters, Sr

The Year of the Poet II
April 2015

Celebrating International Poetry Month

Our Featured Poets

Raja Williams * Dennis Ferado * Laure Charazac

Diamonds

The Poetry Posse 2015
Jamie Bond * Gail Weston Shazor * Albert 'Infinite' Carrasco
Siddartha Beth Pierce * Janet P. Caldwell * Tony Henninger
Joe DaVerbal Minddancer * Neetu Wali * Shareef Abdur – Rasheed
Kimberly Burnham * Ann White * Keith Alan Hamilton
Katherine Wyatt * Fahredin Shehu * Hülya N. Yılmaz
Teresa E. Gallion * Jackie Allen * William S. Peters, Sr

Now Available

www.innerchildpress.com/the-year-of-the-poet

The Year of the Poet II
May 2015

May's Featured Poets

Geri Algeri
Akin Mosi Chinners
Anna Jakubez

Emeralds

The Poetry Posse 2015
Jamie Bond * Gail Weston Shazor * Albert 'Infinite' Carrasco
Siddartha Beth Pierce * Janet P. Caldwell * Tony Henninger
Joe DaVerbal Minddancer * Neetu Wali * Shareef Abdur – Rasheed
Kimberly Burnham * Ann White * Keith Alan Hamilton
Katherine Wyatt * Fahredin Shehu * Hülya N. Yılmaz
Teresa E. Gallion * Jackie Allen * William S. Peters, Sr.

The Year of the Poet II
June 2015

June's Featured Poets

Anahit Arustamyan * Yvette D. Murrell * Regina A. Walker

Pearl

The Poetry Posse 2015
Jamie Bond * Gail Weston Shazor * Albert 'Infinite' Carrasco
Siddartha Beth Pierce * Janet P. Caldwell * Tony Henninger
Joe DaVerbal Minddancer * Neetu Wali * Shareef Abdur – Rasheed
Kimberly Burnham * Ann White * Keith Alan Hamilton
Katherine Wyatt * Fahredin Shehu * Hülya N. Yılmaz
Teresa E. Gallion * Jackie Allen * William S. Peters, Sr

The Year of the Poet II
July 2015

The Featured Poets for July 2015
Abhik Shome * Christina Neal * Robert Neal

Rubies

The Poetry Posse 2015
Jamie Bond * Gail Weston Shazor * Albert 'Infinite' Carrasco
Siddartha Beth Pierce * Janet P. Caldwell * Tony Henninger
Joe DaVerbal Minddancer * Neetu Wali * Shareef Abdur – Rasheed
Kimberly Burnham * Ann White * Keith Alan Hamilton
Katherine Wyatt * Fahredin Shehu * Hülya N. Yılmaz
Teresa E. Gallion * Jackie Allen * William S. Peters, Sr.

The Year of the Poet II
August 2015

Peridot

Featured Poets
Gayle Howell
Ann Chalasz
Christopher Schultz

The Poetry Posse 2015
Jamie Bond * Gail Weston Shazor * Albert 'Infinite' Carrasco
Siddartha Beth Pierce * Janet P. Caldwell * Tony Henninger
Joe DaVerbal Minddancer * Neetu Wali * Shareef Abdur – Rasheed
Kimberly Burnham * Ann White * Keith Alan Hamilton
Katherine Wyatt * Fahredin Shehu * Hülya N. Yılmaz
Teresa E. Gallion * Jackie Allen * William S. Peters, Sr

Now Available

www.innerchildpress.com/the-year-of-the-poet

The Year of the Poet II
September 2015

Featured Poets
Alfreda Ghee * Lonneice Weeks Badley * Demetrios Trifiatis

Sapphires

The Poetry Posse 2015

Jamie Bond * Gail Weston Shazor * Albert 'Infinite' Carrasco
Siddartha Beth Pierce * Janet P. Caldwell * Tony Henninger
Joe DaVerbal Minddancer * Neetu Wali * Shareef Abdur – Rasheed
Kimberly Burnham * Ann White * Keith Alan Hamilton
Katherine Wyatt * Fahredin Shehu * Hülya N. Yılmaz
Teresa E. Gallion * Jackie Allen * William S. Peters, Sr.

The Year of the Poet II
October 2015

Featured Poets
Monte Smith * Laura J. Wolfe * William Washington

Opal

The Poetry Posse 2015

Jamie Bond * Gail Weston Shazor * Albert 'Infinite' Carrasco
Siddartha Beth Pierce * Janet P. Caldwell * Tony Henninger
Joe DaVerbal Minddancer * Neetu Wali * Shareef Abdur – Rasheed
Kimberly Burnham * Ann White * Keith Alan Hamilton
Katherine Wyatt * Fahredin Shehu * Hülya N. Yılmaz
Teresa E. Gallion * Jackie Allen * William S. Peters, Sr.

The Year of the Poet II
November 2015

Featured Poets
Alan W. Jankowski
Bismay Mohanty
James Moore

Topaz

The Poetry Posse 2015

Jamie Bond * Gail Weston Shazor * Albert 'Infinite' Carrasco
Siddartha Beth Pierce * Janet P. Caldwell * Tony Henninger
Joe DaVerbal Minddancer * Neetu Wali * Shareef Abdur – Rasheed
Kimberly Burnham * Ann White * Keith Alan Hamilton
Katherine Wyatt * Fahredin Shehu * Hülya N. Yılmaz
Teresa E. Gallion * Jackie Allen * William S. Peters, Sr.

The Year of the Poet II
December 2015

Featured Poets
Kerione Bryan * Michelle Joan Barulich * Neville Hiatt

Turquoise

The Poetry Posse 2015

Jamie Bond * Gail Weston Shazor * Albert 'Infinite' Carrasco
Siddartha Beth Pierce * Janet P. Caldwell * Tony Henninger
Joe DaVerbal Minddancer * Neetu Wali * Shareef Abdur – Rasheed
Kimberly Burnham * Ann White * Keith Alan Hamilton
Katherine Wyatt * Fahredin Shehu * Hülya N. Yılmaz
Teresa E. Gallion * Jackie Allen * William S. Peters, Sr.

Now Available

www.innerchildpress.com/the-year-of-the-poet

The Year of the Poet III
January 2016

Featured Poets

Lana Joseph * Atoni Cyrus Rush * Christena Williams

Dark-eyed Junco

The Poetry Posse 2016

The Year of the Poet III
February 2016

Featured Poets
Anthony Arnold
Anna Chalasz
Andre Hawthorne

Puffin

The Poetry Posse 2016

The Year of the Poet
March 2016
Featured Poets

Jeton Kelmendi   Nizar Sartawi   Sami Muhanna

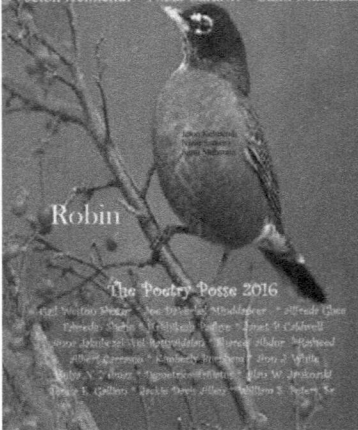

Robin

The Poetry Posse 2016

The Year of the Poet III

Featured Poets

Ali Abdolrezaei

Anna Chalasz

Agim Vinca

Ceri Naz

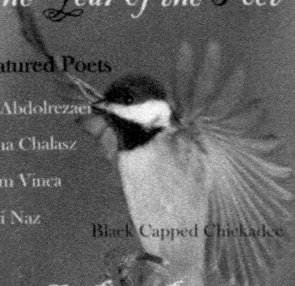

Black Capped Chickadee

The Poetry Posse 2016

celebrating international poetry month

Now Available

www.innerchildpress.com/the-year-of-the-poet

The Year of the Poet
May 2016

Bob Strum
Barbara Allan
D.L. Davis

Oriole

The Year of the Poet III
June 2016

Featured Poets

Qibrije Demiri- Frangu
Naime Beqiraj
Faleeha Hassan
Bedri Zyberaj

Black Necked Stilt

The Poetry Posse 2016

The Year of the Poet
July

Iram Fatima 'Ashi'
Langley Shazor
Jody Doty
Emilia T. Davis

Indigo Bunting

The Poetry Posse 2016

The Year of the Poet III
August 2016

Featured Poets

Anita Dash
Irena Jovanovic
Malgorzata Gouluda

Painted Bunting

The Poetry Posse 2016

Now Available

www.innerchildpress.com/the-year-of-the-poet

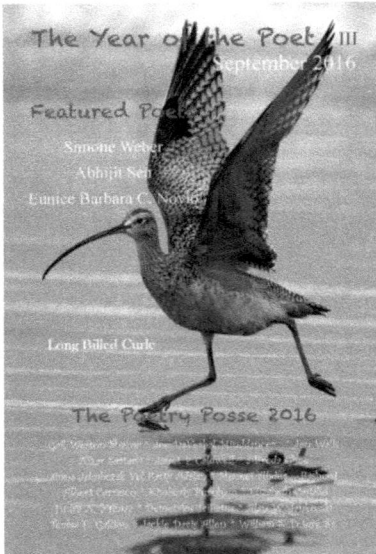

The Year of the Poet III
September 2016

Featured Poets

Simone Weber
Abhijit Sen
Eunice Barbara C. Novio

Long Billed Curle

The Poetry Posse 2016

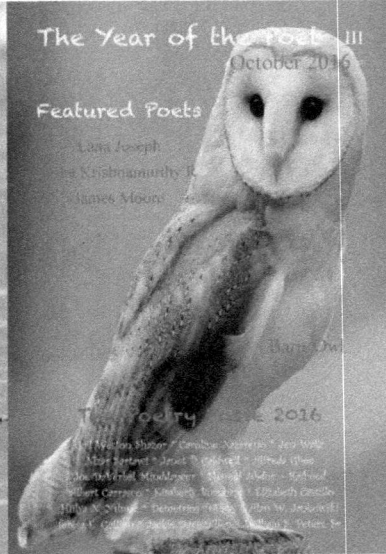

The Year of the Poet III
October 2016

Featured Poets

Lana Joseph
Krishnamurthy
James Moore

Barn Owl

The Poetry Posse 2016

The Year of the Poet III
November 2016

Featured Poets

Rosemary Burns
Robin Ouzman Hislop
Lonneice Weeks-Badler

Northern Cardinal

The Poetry Posse 2016

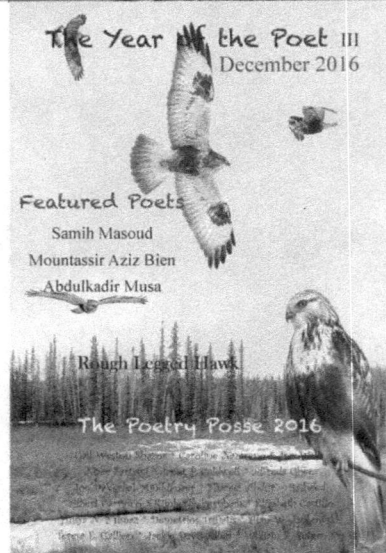

The Year of the Poet III
December 2016

Featured Poets

Samih Masoud
Mountassir Aziz Bien
Abdulkadir Musa

Rough Legged Hawk

The Poetry Posse 2016

Now Available

www.innerchildpress.com/the-year-of-the-poet

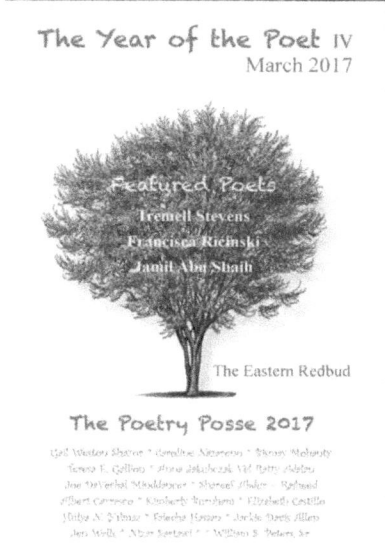

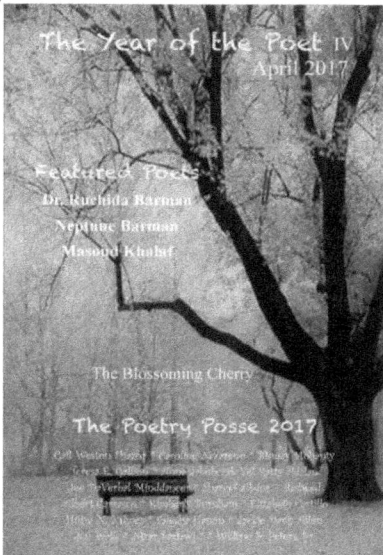

The Year of the Poet IV
January 2017

The Year of the Poet IV
February 2017

The Year of the Poet IV
March 2017

The Year of the Poet IV
April 2017

Now Available

www.innerchildpress.com/the-year-of-the-poet

The Year of the Poet IV
May 2017

The Flowering Dogwood Tree

Featured Poets
Kallisa Powell
Alicja Maria Kuberska
Fethi Sassi

The Poetry Posse 2017

Gail Weston Shazor * Caroline Nazareno * Shixuy Mohanty
Teresa E. Gallion * Anna Jakubczak Val Betty Adelm
Joe DaVerbal Minddancer * Shareef Abdur - Rasheed
Albert Carrasco * Kimberly Burnham * Elizabeth Castillo
Hülya N. Yilmaz * Peleche Hessms * Jackie Davis Allen
Jen Walls * Nizar Sartawi * * William S. Peters, Sr.

The Year of the Poet IV
June 2017

Featured Poets
Eliza Segiet
Tze-Min Tsai
Abdulla Issa

The Linden Tree

The Poetry Posse 2017

Hülya N. Yilmaz * Caroline Nazareno
Jen Walls * Nizar Sartawi * William S. Peters

The Year of the Poet IV
July 2017

Featured Poets
Anca Mihaela Bruma
Ibaa Ismail
Zvonko Taneski

The Oak Moon

The Poetry Posse 2017

The Year of the Poet IV
August 2017

Featured Poets
Jonathan Aquino
Kitty Hsu
Langley Shazor

The Hazelnut Tree

The Poetry Posse 2017

Gail Weston Shazor * Caroline Nazareno *
Teresa E. Gallion * Anna Jakubczak Val Betty Adelm
Joe DaVerbal Minddancer * Shareef Abdur - Rasheed
Albert Carrasco * Kimberly Burnham * Elizabeth Castillo
Hülya N. Yilmaz * Peleche Hessms * Jackie Davis Allen
Jen Walls * Nizar Sartawi * * William S. Peters, Sr.

Now Available

www.innerchildpress.com/the-year-of-the-poet

The Year of the Poet IV
September 2017

Featured Poets
Martina Reisz Newberry
Ameer Nassir
Christine Fulco Neal
Robert Neal

The Elm Tree

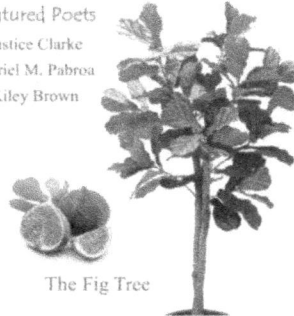

The Poetry Posse 2017

Gail Weston Shazor * Caroline Nazareno * Bismay Mohanty
Teresa E. Gallion * Anna Jakubczak Vel Ratty Adalan
Joe DaVerbal Minddancer * Shareef Abdur – Rasheed
Albert Carrasco * Kimberly Burnham * Elizabeth Castillo
Hülya N. Yılmaz * Faleeha Hassan * Jackie Davis Allen
Jen Walls * Nizar Sartawi * * William S. Peters, Sr.

The Year of the Poet IV
October 2017

Featured Poets
Ahmed Abu Saleem
Nedal Al-Qaeim
Sadeddin Shahin

The Black Walnut Tree

The Poetry Posse 2017

Gail Weston Shazor * Caroline Nazareno * Bismay Mohanty
Teresa E. Gallion * Anna Jakubczak Vel Ratty Adalan
Joe DaVerbal Minddancer * Shareef Abdur – Rasheed
Albert Carrasco * Kimberly Burnham * Elizabeth Castillo
Hülya N. Yılmaz * Faleeha Hassan * Jackie Davis Allen
Jen Walls * Nizar Sartawi * * William S. Peters, Sr.

The Year of the Poet IV
November 2017

Featured Poets
Kay Peters
Alfreda D. Ghee
Gabriella Garofalo
Rosemary Cappello

The Tree of Life

The Poetry Posse 2017

Gail Weston Shazor * Caroline Nazareno * Bismay Mohanty
Teresa E. Gallion * Anna Jakubczak Vel Ratty Adalan
Joe DaVerbal Minddancer * Shareef Abdur – Rasheed
Albert Carrasco * Kimberly Burnham * Elizabeth Castillo
Hülya N. Yılmaz * Faleeha Hassan * Jackie Davis Allen
Jen Walls * Nizar Sartawi * William S. Peters, Sr.

The Year of the Poet IV
December 2017

Featured Poets
Justice Clarke
Mariel M. Pabroa
Kiley Brown

The Fig Tree

The Poetry Posse 2017

Gail Weston Shazor * Caroline Nazareno * Bismay Mohanty
Teresa E. Gallion * Anna Jakubczak Vel Ratty Adalan
Joe DaVerbal Minddancer * Shareef Abdur – Rasheed
Albert Carrasco * Kimberly Burnham * Elizabeth Castillo
Hülya N. Yılmaz * Faleeha Hassan * Jackie Davis Allen
Jen Walls * Nizar Sartawi * William S. Peters, Sr.

Now Available

www.innerchildpress.com/the-year-of-the-poet

The Year of the Poet V
January 2018
Featured Poets
Iyad Shamasnah
Yasmeen Hamzeh
Ali Abdolrezaei

Aksum

The Poetry Posse 2018
Gail Weston Shazor * Caroline Nazareno * Tezmin Ition Tsai
Hülya N. Yılmaz * Faleeha Hassan * Jackie Davis Allen
Teresa E. Gallion * Anna Jakubczak Vel Ratty Adalan
Alicja Maria Kuberska * Shareef Abdur – Rasheed
Kimberly Burnham * Elizabeth Castillo
Nizar Sartawi * William S. Peters, Sr.

The Year of the Poet V
February 2018
Sabean
Featured Poets
Muhammad Azram
Anna Szawracka
Abhilipsa Kuanar
Aanika Aery

The Poetry Posse 2018
Gail Weston Shazor * Caroline Nazareno * Tezmin Ition Tsai
Hülya N. Yılmaz * Faleeha Hassan * Jackie Davis Allen
Teresa E. Gallion * Anna Jakubczak Vel Ratty Adalan
Alicja Maria Kuberska * Shareef Abdur – Rasheed
Kimberly Burnham * Elizabeth Castillo
Nizar Sartawi * William S. Peters, Sr.

The Year of the Poet V
March 2018
Featured Poets
Iram Fatima 'Ashi'
Cassandra Swan
Jaleel Khazaal
Shazia Zaman

Caribbean
&
Middle America

The Poetry Posse 2018
Gail Weston Shazor * Nizar Sartawi * Hülya N. Yılmaz
Jackie Davis Allen * Caroline 'Ceri' Nazareno
Alicja Maria Kuberska * Teresa E. Gallion
Faleeha Hassan * Shareef Abdur – Rasheed
Kimberly Burnham * Elizabeth Castillo
Tezmin Ition Tsai * William S. Peters, Sr.

The Year of the Poet V
April 2018
Featured Poets

The Nez Perce

The Poetry Posse 2018

Now Available

www.innerchildpress.com/the-year-of-the-poet

The Year of the Poet V
May 2018

Featured Poets

The Sumerians

The Poetry Posse 2018

Gail Weston Shazor * Nizar Sartawi * Hülya N. Yılmaz
Jackie Davis Allen * Caroline 'Ceri' Nazareno
Alicja Maria Kuberska * Teresa E. Gallion
Kimberly Burnham * Shareef Abdur – Rasheed
Faleeha Hassan * Elizabeth Castillo * Swapna Behera
Tezmin Ition Tsai * William S. Peters, Sr.

The Year of the Poet V
June 2018

Featured Poets
Bilal Mrizqi * Dijun Miftari * Gojko Božović * Sofija Živković

The Paleo Indians

The Poetry Posse 2018

The Year of the Poet V
July 2018

Featured Poets
Fatimah Ireneae-Paddy
Mohammad Akbal Harb
Eliza Segiet
Tom Higgins

Oceania

The Poetry Posse 2018

Gail Weston Shazor * Nizar Sartawi * Hülya N. Yılmaz
Jackie Davis Allen * Caroline 'Ceri' Nazareno
Alicja Maria Kuberska * Teresa E. Gallion
Kimberly Burnham * Shareef Abdur – Rasheed
Faleeha Hassan * Elizabeth Castillo * Swapna Behera
Tezmin Ition Tsai * William S. Peters, Sr.

The Year of the Poet V
August 2018

Featured Poets
Hussein Habasch * Mircea Dan Duta * Nada Mujkić * Swagat Das

The Lapita

The Poetry Posse 2018

Gail Weston Shazor * Nizar Sartawi * Hülya N. Yılmaz
Jackie Davis Allen * Caroline 'Ceri' Nazareno
Alicja Maria Kuberska * Teresa E. Gallion
Kimberly Burnham * Shareef Abdur – Rasheed
Ashok K. Bhargava * Elizabeth Castillo * Swapna Behera
Tezmin Ition Tsai * William S. Peters, Sr.

Now Available

www.innerchildpress.com/the-year-of-the-poet

and there is much, much more !

visit . . .

http://www.innerchildpress.com
/anthologies-sales-special.php

Also check out our Authors and
all the wonderful Books
Available at :

http://www.innerchildpress.com
/the-book-store.php

INNER CHILD PRESS

WORLD HEALING WORLD PEACE
2018

A Poetry Anthology for Humanity

Now Available

www.worldhealingworldpeacepoetry.com

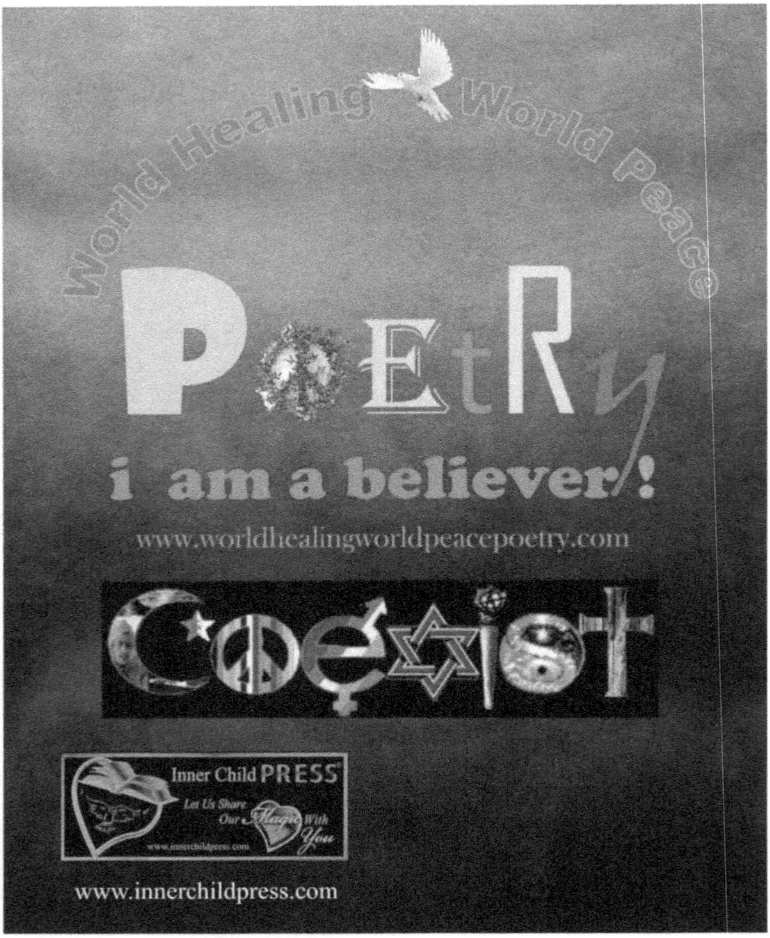

Now Available

www.worldhealingworldpeacepoetry.com

Support
World Healing
World Peace

www.worldhealingworldpeacepoetry.com

175

World Healing
World Peace
2018

Now Available

www.worldhealingworldpeacepoetry.com

Inner Child Press International

'building cultural bridges of understanding'

Meet the Board of Directors

William S. Peters, Sr.
Chair Person
Founder
Inner Child Enterprises
Inner Child Press

Hülya N Yılmaz
Director
Editing Services
Co-Chair Person

Nizar Sartawi
Director
International
Relations

Fahredin B. Shehu
Director
Cultural Affairs

Gail Weston Shazor
Director
Anthologies

Kimberly Burnham
Director
Cultural Ambassador
Pacific Northwest
USA

Deborah Smart
Director
Publicity
Marketing

De'Andre Hawthorne
Director
Performance Poetry

Ashok K. Bhargava
Director
WIN Awards

www.innerchildpress.com

nner Child Press International

'building cultural bridges of understanding'

Meet our Cultural Ambassadors

Fahredin Shehu
Director of Cultural
International

Faleha Hassan
Iraq ~ USA

Elizabeth E. Castillo
Philippines

Kimberly Burnham
Pacific Northwest
USA

Alicja Kuberska
Poland
Eastern Europe

Swapna Behera
India
Southeast Asia

Ashok K. Bhargava
Canada

Tzemin Ition Tsai
Republic of China
Greater China

Laure Charazac
France
Western Europe

www.innerchildpress.com

178

This Anthological Publication
is underwritten solely by

Inner Child Press

Inner Child Press is a Publishing Company
Founded and Operated by Writers. Our personal
publishing experiences provides us an intimate
understanding of the sometimes daunting
challenges Writers, New and Seasoned may face in
the Business of Publishing and Marketing their
Creative "Written Work".

For more Information

Inner Child Press

www.innerchildpress.com

Inner Child PRESS

Let Us Share
Our *Magic* With
You

www.innerchildpress.com

~ *fini* ~

www.ingramcontent.com/pod-product-compliance
Lightning Source LLC
LaVergne TN
LVHW011156080426
835508LV00007B/443